TRIPLE ALLIANCE
AND
TRIPLE ENTENTE

BY

BERNADOTTE E. SCHMITT

NEW YORK

Howard Fertig

1971

HOWARD FERTIG, INC. EDITION 1971
Reprinted by arrangement with Holt, Rinehart and Winston, Inc.

Library of Congress Catalog Card Number: 70-80590

PRINTED IN THE UNITED STATES OF AMERICA
BY NOBLE OFFSET PRINTERS, INC.

CONTENTS

vii

PAGE

TRIPLE ALLIANCE
AND
TRIPLE ENTENTE

This d—d system of alliances, which were the curse of modern times.
> ARTHUR ZIMMERMANN, undersecretary of state
> in the German foreign office, 1 August, 1914.

Whatever we may think of the merits of the Austrian charges against Servia, France and Russia consider that these are the pretexts, and the bigger cause of Triple Alliance versus Triple *Entente* is definitely engaged.
> SIR EYRE CROWE, assistant undersecretary of
> state in the British foreign office, 25 July,
> 1914.

I have decided on these advances towards the point of view of Italy because we are playing a great game, in which there are serious difficulties to overcome, and in which we might fail, unless the Powers of the Triple Alliance hold firmly together.
> COUNT BERCHTOLD, Austro-Hungarian minister
> of foreign affairs, 28 July, 1914.

No single outstanding fact caused the war, really the graver blame rested upon the whole European system, a concatenation of alliances and treaties, a complicated network of intrigue and espionage which unerringly caught the entire family in its meshes.
> WOODROW WILSON, 16 October, 1916.

THE WORLD WAR was precipitated by the murder of the Archduke Francis Ferdinand at Sarajevo on 28 June, 1914, for the crime brought to a head a long-smouldering quarrel between Austria-Hungary and Serbia. In this quarrel Russia and Italy might reasonably have been expected to interfere, Russia because she had often posed as the protector of her Slavic kins-

1

men in the Balkans, Italy because she had long been suspicious of Austro-Hungarian activity in the Balkans which might threaten the equilibrium of the Adriatic. But it can hardly be said that the direct interests of Germany, France and Great Britain were involved in the Austro-Serbian dispute. Yet these three Powers were promptly drawn into the war which began between Austria-Hungary and Serbia on 28 July, 1914. The explanation of this fact is distressingly simple: Germany was the ally of Austria-Hungary, France was the ally of Russia, and Great Britain was bound to France by a diplomatic agreement which, though not technically and formally an alliance, was found to have the "moral obligation" of an alliance. "No one can escape his destiny," said the Russian minister of the interior as he countersigned the order for the mobilization of the Russian army. Yet there can be no doubt that the alliances were originally intended to prevent the very catastrophe which overwhelmed Europe in 1914. It is the purpose of this little book to show how the alliances came into being and how their pacific purposes were modified and deflected until they became veritable instruments of war.

I

THE TRIPLE ALLIANCE

EUROPE AFTER 1871

In 1870 the unification of Italy, begun by Cavour in 1859, was practically completed by the occupation of Rome; only Trentino and the city of Trieste remained to be won. In 1871 the German Empire was established by Bismarck, and the Treaty of Frankfort, which ended the war between France and Germany, provided for the cession of Alsace and part of Lorraine to Germany. In 1878 the Treaty of Berlin, which followed on the Russo-Turkish war of 1877, secured the independence or autonomy of various Balkan states. It was on the basis of these territorial arrangements, which lasted, so far as western Europe was concerned, until 1914 and were not disturbed in the Balkans until 1912-13, that the "d—d system of alliances" was conceived and developed.

During these forty-three years the dominant position in European politics was held by Germany. Her location in the centre of the continent gave her a great advantage if she wished to exert pressure on other Powers, and her army, which had been victorious in three wars against Denmark, Austria and France successively, remained the most formidable military machine in the world, even after the other continental states had adopted her practice of universal military service. In short, no Power was in a position to challenge Germany single-handed, nor, for long years, could any important decision be taken without her participation and approval. On the other hand, precisely because of her central location, Germany would be exposed to serious danger if her neighbors to the east and west combined against her. This was not likely to happen so long as Germany was content with the frontiers secured in 1871, and Bismarck, who remained in power until 1890, never tired of proclaiming that Germany was "saturated." Nevertheless the great chancellor realized keenly that the diplomatic methods he had employed against Denmark, Austria and France had aroused deep discontent and suspicion; other governments could not altogether overcome the fear that he might some day use them again. In other words, it behooved Germany to walk warily and instead of relying on her great strength to antagonize other Powers, to bind as many of them as possible to a conservative policy controlled by herself.

Bismarck was unquestionably the greatest diplomatist of his day. His skill lay not so much in his complete mastery of the technique of international politics or his capacity for detecting the weaknesses of his opponents as in the possession of certain qualities which his successors conspicuously lacked. First of all, he knew what he wanted and he could estimate to a nicety how far he could go without danger. Secondly, he had a keen appreciation of the legitimate interests of other nations and allowed for them in his

own calculations. But most valuable of all was his
resourcefulness in difficult moments. The more critical
a situation became, the more energetically did Bismarck exert himself to master it, and usually with success. He was not content to approach a problem by
one route only: there was always at least one alternative course, and towards the end of his career he was
like a juggler who plays with four or five balls. Some
of his work has been subjected to criticism which, in
the light of subsequent events and present perspective,
is not unjustified; but it is only fair to remember that
Bismarck was removed from office at a critical moment and that one important feature of his policy was
immediately discarded. Up to the hour of his fall, he
continued to dominate European politics with his usual
vigor, although his manœuvres had become increasingly
complicated. His ascendency is also to be explained
partly by the fact that for twenty years he exercised
an absolute control over Germany's policy, whereas in
other countries not only did foreign ministers frequently change, but they were often subjected to popular parliamentary or court influences from which Bismarck was happily freed or which he ignored. It is
perhaps a measure of Bismarck's stature that he negotiated most easily and readily with men who had some
of his own downrightness and strength. He had the
greatest admiration for Disraeli, whom he called "the
man" of the Berlin Congress, and he always got on
very well with Salisbury, who did not mince his words.
If he found that he could manipulate men, Bismarck
manipulated them; if they stood up to him, he treated

them with respect and consideration. If he ruled Europe somewhat tyrannically at times, at least he kept a greater degree of order than any statesman since Metternich, and the removal of his strong hand left a gap that was never filled.

Throughout the period from 1871 to 1890, Bismarck's aim was to preserve the position of the new German Empire, and while he was ready to fight if necessary, his policy was fundamentally one of peace. The execution of this policy, though it became more and more complex with the passing years, was governed by one elementary fact: the refusal of France to recognize the Treaty of Frankfort as morally binding. The French carried out the treaty to the letter, but their desire to avenge the military defeat and to recover the lost provinces manifested itself in many forms. Since the representatives of Alsace-Lorraine had protested to both the French national assembly at Bordeaux and the German Reichstag against the transfer of the provinces, the French attitude was logical. In Bismarck's opinion, the French could not be expected to forgive or forget, and he assumed that they would attack Germany when a favorable opportunity presented itself. But he was also persuaded that in view of Germany's military superiority, they would do so only if they could secure an ally—which could be only Russia or Austria-Hungary. From first to last, therefore, his guiding principle was to prevent France from securing that ally.

The first step was taken in 1872 by the formation of the Three Emperors' League. The Emperor Francis

Joseph of Austria and the Tsar Alexander II visited
Berlin and there informally (i.e., nothing was put in
writing) agreed with the German Emperor that the
status quo must be preserved and revolutionary ideas
suppressed.[1] In the following year the King of Italy
also came to Berlin and announced his adherence to
the League. As Great Britain was not at this time
pursuing an active policy in continental affairs, republican France was left isolated.

THE "SCARE" OF 1875

Actually, the Three Emperors' League soon proved
a disappointment. Bismarck had been greatly annoyed
by the manifestations of sympathy on the part of the
French bishops for the Catholic clergy of Prussia during the *Kulturkampf,* and he thought that the time had
come to impress the French with a sense of their isolation. When, therefore, the French parliament in the
spring of 1875 passed a law adding a fourth battalion
to each regiment of the army, the German chancellor
professed to regard this as the signal of an impending
attack by France. A Berlin newspaper published a
sensational article entitled "Is War in Sight?"—which
did not lose in effect from the rumors, which were

[1] In 1873 Germany and Russia signed a military convention by
which they promised each other the assistance of 200,000 troops if
either was attacked. Shortly afterwards, Austria-Hungary and Russia
entered into an agreement that "in case an aggression from a third
Power should compromise the peace of Europe," they would "come
to an understanding between themselves, without seeking or contracting new alliances, in order to agree as to the line of conduct to be
followed in common."

correct, that the German general staff was urging a "preventive" war. The chief of staff, Field Marshal von Moltke, used threatening language to the Belgian minister in Berlin, and the German government sent a stiff note to Paris. The French foreign minister, the Duke Decazes, cleverly seized the chance to score off Bismarck. Pretending to be greatly alarmed, he appealed to the Tsar, and that monarch, accompanied by his chancellor, Prince Gorchakov, made a visit to Berlin. The British government had also been warned by Decazes, and Queen Victoria wrote a letter to the Emperor William. As a result the crisis was quickly ended. Nevertheless, the consequences were important.

Bismarck always denied that he had contemplated war with France and laid the blame for the "scare" on the intrigues of Gorchakov. To this day historians are not agreed as to what were the German chancellor's real intentions. But whatever they were, he had learned that the other Powers were not disposed to allow Germany to crush France a second time and that even an isolated France was not friendless. The French, for their part, always believed that Bismarck had meant war and never lost an opportunity to make capital out of the incident. It is probable that Decazes had much more to do with the scare than Gorchakov, but Bismarck held that Gorchakov had quite needlessly disturbed the harmony of the Three Emperors' League, and early in 1876 he made overtures to Great Britain for an alliance.

THE CRISIS IN THE NEAR EAST, 1875-1878

The emotions produced by this "scare" had hardly subsided when a serious crisis broke out in the Near East. In July, 1875, the inhabitants of Bosnia and Herzegovina, two Turkish provinces lying along the southwestern border of Austria-Hungary, rebelled against their Turkish masters, and in the spring of 1876 Serbia and Montenegro, disgusted by the failure of European diplomacy to deal adequately with the situation and anxious themselves to fish in the troubled waters, went to war with Turkey—only to be defeated. The Bulgarians had also risen against the Turks, and had been savagely repressed. Russian public opinion was deeply stirred by these events and began to clamor for intervention. Such a possibility greatly alarmed the Austrian government, which was unwilling to see Russian influence extended in the Balkans and also feared the effect of Russian action on its own Slavic subjects. Although the Emperor Francis Joseph and the Tsar Alexander II had met in June and worked out a policy of quasi-coöperation (agreement of Reichstadt), it was soon evident that the Three Emperors' League was a broken reed. In Russia the Pan-Slavists conducted so violent an agitation against Austria-Hungary, which they regarded as the main obstacle to the realization of their dreams, that in the autumn the Tsar was constrained to inquire of Bismarck if Germany would remain neutral in an Austro-Russian war. This was an exceedingly awkward question for Bismarck, for it forced him to choose between Austria and Russia. To answer the question in the sense desired by Russia would probably mean the end of Austria— and Bismarck always regarded the maintenance of the Habsburg state as a primary German interest, for otherwise Germany would be left to face Russia alone. Yet a reply in the negative might throw Russia into the arms of France. The German chancellor therefore sought to evade the issue by suggesting the possibility of an agreement if Russia would guarantee the possession of Alsace-Lorraine to Germany. But the Russians refused to take this seriously and renewed their question. Pressed into a corner, Bismarck finally replied that his first care had always been to preserve friendship between the monarchies as the best guarantee against revolution; but "if, to our sorrow, this was not possible between Russia and Austria, then we could endure indeed that our friends should lose or win battles against each other, but not that one of the two should be so severely wounded and injured that its position as an independent Great Power taking its part in the councils of Europe would be endangered." The meaning of this language was perfectly clear: Bismarck had chosen for Austria, and the decision governed his policy for the rest of his career. The Russians understood it so well that they gave up the idea of a war against Austria in favor of a war with Turkey, struck a bargain with the cabinet of Vienna on the conditions of Austrian neutrality,[2] and opened war against Turkey in April, 1877.

[2] Convention of Budapest (secret), 15 January, 1877. Austria agreed to observe benevolent neutrality and to try to prevent intervention or

But if Bismarck had been unwilling to give Russia
a free hand against Austria, he also resisted the pressure from Austria to restrain Russia from attacking
Turkey. He took the position that Russia had legitimate interests in the Near East, and he did not propose
to compromise the traditional friendship of Germany
and Russia by opposing the latter's ambitions at the
behest of Austria. He endeavored, he said, to act as
"an honest broker" between the two rivals. He could
do this because, as he declared in a famous speech, the
Eastern question "involved no German interest which
would be worth the bones of a single Pomeranian gren-
adier." This attitude he maintained to the end of his
career. Moreover, believing the Ottoman Empire not
to be worth preserving, he desired the other Powers,
instead of fighting over the Turkish heritage, to agree
in advance on the lines of partition and to appropriate
their shares at opportune moments. Russia, in his
opinion, should dominate the eastern, while Austria-
Hungary should control the western Balkans; Great
Britain should occupy Egypt and Suez and negotiate
with Russia concerning Constantinople; France might
be assigned Syria; even Italy could have something.
The compensation for Germany would be that some
such compromise would obviate the necessity of diplomatic combinations or the danger of war which might
threaten the central position of Germany; to be more
precise, so long as Austria and Russia did not quarrel

collective mediation by other powers; she reserved the right to occupy
Bosnia and Herzegovina when she saw fit. In return, Russia promised not to create a large state, Slavic or other, in the Balkans.

violently, neither would be disposed to seek the alliance of France. Bismarck never tired of letting his views be known to other governments, but unfortunately they were too suspicious of each other, and perhaps also of Bismarck, to listen to his advice.

The Russo-Turkish war which began in April, 1877, was ended disastrously for Turkey by the Treaty of San Stefano on 3 March, 1878. According to this instrument, Rumania, Serbia, and Montenegro were recognized as independent; an autonomous principality of Bulgaria was erected, stretching from the Black Sea to the mountains of Albania and including a stretch of Ægean seacoast; certain reforms were promised in Bosnia-Herzegovina; Russia was to acquire large districts in Asia Minor and a sizable indemnity from Turkey. The treaty to a very considerable degree realized the Pan-Slavic programme of Orthodox Russia and provided for the expulsion of the Turks "bag and baggage" from most of their European territories. It at once aroused vehement protest. Austria complained that it violated the conditions under which she had agreed to remain neutral; for it established a large Slavic state in the Balkans and it maintained Turkish sovereignty over Bosnia-Herzegovina. Great Britain objected to the practical partition of the Ottoman Empire and the ascendency of Russia in the Balkans, and proceeded to take military measures, including the despatch of her fleet to Constantinople. Both Powers demanded that Russia submit the entire treaty to a congress of the powers, and signed an agreement to work together. Russia was exceedingly reluctant to accept any revision of the treaty. For a time it seemed that a general war might result. To prevent this Bismarck advised Russia to submit the treaty to revision, thereby a second time acting for Austria and against Russia. In these circumstances Russia had to yield.

The Congress of Berlin, which sat from 13 June to 13 July, 1878, was the last full-dress gathering of the "old" European diplomacy. Attended by the first ministers of Germany, Russia, Austria and Great Britain and the most experienced diplomatists of other states and presided over by Bismarck in masterful fashion, it quickly revised the Treaty of San Stefano. By the Treaty of Berlin, Bulgaria was greatly reduced in size and the Turkish Empire in Europe reconstituted; Russia surrendered some of her acquisitions in Asia Minor; Austria was empowered to "occupy and administer" Bosnia-Herzegovina. Great Britain, by a separate agreement with Turkey, was allowed to occupy and administer the island of Cyprus. Thus, with the assistance of Bismarck, Great Britain and Austria reduced the Russian influence in the Near East and paid themselves handsomely without firing a shot. At the Congress Bismarck often supported the Russians, but on the large issues he stood by Great Britain and Austria, and when the Russians subsequently asserted that their humiliation was due to Bismarck, they were but stating the fact. The German chancellor justified his policy on the ground that it had saved the peace of Europe; incidentally it marked a step towards the partition of the Ottoman Empire by agreement.

THE AUSTRO-GERMAN ALLIANCE, 1879

In the year following the Berlin Congress Russian resentment towards Germany manifested itself in a variety of ways. Not only did the press indulge in violent polemics, but the minister of war began to concentrate troops along the Russo-German frontier. Finally the Tsar wrote a bitter letter to the Emperor William complaining that in the complicated negotiations arising out of the application of the Berlin treaty, the German representatives were voting against Russia; Alexander declared that Germany must change her ways if the old friendship with Russia were to continue. Bismarck accordingly decided in August, 1879, that the time had come for a fundamental change in German policy: the Three Emperors' League having been killed by the Austro-Russian rivalry in the Balkans, Germany, now that she was faced by open Russian hostility, had no alternative but to ally herself with Austria. A further incentive was the fact that Russia was reported to be making overtures to France and Italy. The German Emperor, who was the uncle of the Tsar, agreed to the negotiations with Austria only with the greatest reluctance and stipulated that any alliance must be general in character and not directed against Russia.

The Austro-Hungarian foreign minister, Count Andrássy, had never been enthusiastic about the Three Emperors' League; he would have much preferred an alliance with Germany only. Realizing that he now had Bismarck at a disadvantage, he refused the German chancellor's proposals for a general defensive alliance directed against aggression by any Power or Powers and reinforced by constitutional guarantees. He indicated that Austria was not willing to bind herself against France and stipulated for an alliance against Russia. Bismarck readily agreed to this, but he had great difficulty in persuading his imperial master to accept it. William threatened to abdicate, Bismarck to resign. In the end, Bismarck had to mobilize the Crown Prince, the chief of staff General von Moltke, and the entire German and Prussian governments (they were prepared to resign) before the Emperor capitulated.

The treaty of alliance between Germany and Austria-Hungary was signed on 7 October, 1879. The principal provisions were:

Article I. Should, contrary to their hope, and against the loyal desire of the two High Contracting Parties, one of the two Empires be attacked by Russia, the High Contracting Parties are bound to come to the assistance one of the other with the whole war strength of their Empires, and accordingly only to conclude peace together and upon mutual agreement.

Article II. Should one of the High Contracting Parties be attacked by another Power, the other High Contracting Party binds itself hereby, not only not to support the aggressor against its high Ally, but to observe at least a benevolent neutral attitude towards its fellow Contracting Party.

Should, however, the attacking party in such a case be supported by Russia, either by an active participation or by military measures which constitute a menace to the Party attacked, then the obligation stipulated in Article I of this Treaty, for reciprocal assistance with the whole fighting force, becomes equally operative, and the conduct of the war by the Two High Contracting Parties shall in this case also be in common until the conclusion of common peace.

The purpose of the treaty, which was to be kept secret, was strictly defensive in both letter and spirit.

This alliance marks a turning-point in the history of Europe. There had often been alliances in the past, but they had usually been concluded for specific purposes and were dissolved when the aim was achieved. This Austro-German alliance, however, was destined to be permanent. Concluded originally for a term of five years, it was renewed in 1883 and again in 1902; it lasted indeed until it collapsed in October, 1918, under the pressure of military defeat. It was destined to be the first in a series of alliances which developed into a system and a counter-system, until finally the six Great Powers found themselves divided into two rival groups of three each.

This was not, of course, foreseen by the statesmen who made the alliance. The Austrian motive was simply to secure German assistance in the event that Austro-Russian rivalry in the Balkans should lead to war; Andrássy refused to be drawn into Germany's quarrel with France. For Bismarck the essential thing was that the alliance gave pause to Russia and preserved the peace of Europe; it also strengthened the position of the Germans in Austria against the rising tide of Slav discontent with the Compromise of 1867, and it restored the tradition of two equal German

Great Powers which had been destroyed in 1866. The Emperor William disliked the alliance because he feared that it would throw Russia into the arms of France, and this did finally happen. Ultimately the alliance also involved Germany in the disastrous Balkan policy of Austria. But both of these developments occurred after the fall of Bismarck. The alliance served its immediate purpose well and was hailed by the British foreign secretary, Lord Salisbury, as "good tidings of great joy." [3]

THE TRIPLE ALLIANCE, 1882

The Austro-German *bloc* was strengthened in 1882 by the adhesion of Italy. For Italy, which was the newest and weakest of the Great Powers, to seek the alliance of Germany, the strongest Power, was natural enough, but that she should ally with Austria, the hereditary enemy, was surprising. The explanation long offered and accepted was that Italy acted out of resentment against France for the establishment of her protectorate over Tunis (1881). Undoubtedly Italian opinion was profoundly annoyed by the French action, but the party of the Left in control of the Italian government was strongly sympathetic with France. The real motive seems to have been a desire to strengthen the position of the Italian government against the Papacy, while the King was alarmed by the

[3] While the negotiations with Austria were under way, Bismarck made overtures to Great Britain for an alliance. The British showed some interest, but Bismarck, for reasons not altogether clear, did not proceed further.

continued evidences of republicanism and wished to establish close relations with the "autocratic" monarchies. The Italians would have preferred to make an alliance with Germany alone, but Bismarck referred them to Vienna. Italy accordingly proposed to Austria a treaty of guarantee, which would ensure the possession of Rome by Italy in the event of trouble with the Pope. As this was refused by Austria, the treaty finally took the form of a defensive alliance, to which Germany was a party. The most important articles of the treaty of 20 May, 1882, were as follows:

Article II. In case Italy, without direct provocation on her part, should be attacked by France for any reason whatsoever, the two other Contracting Parties shall be bound to lend help and assistance with all their forces to the Party attacked.

The same obligation shall evolve upon Italy in case of any aggression without direct provocation by France against Germany.

Article III. If one, or two, of the High Contracting Parties, without provocation on their part, should chance to be attacked and to be engaged in a war with two or more Great Powers nonsignatory to the present treaty, the *casus fœderis* will arise simultaneously for all the High Contracting Parties.

The treaty, which was to be kept secret, was to have a duration of five years. Declarations were exchanged stating that the treaty could not "in any case be regarded as being directed against England."

It will be noted that whereas Italy could claim the help of both her allies if she were attacked, she was bound to help Germany only. Austria did not insist on

Italian help against Russia because she had refused to promise assistance to Germany against France. Moreover, Bismarck, who had a low opinion of the Italians and thought that their military effort, even if it were made, would be of little value, persuaded the Austrian government that the essential thing was to secure Italian neutrality in the event of an Austro-Russian war. The Triple Alliance was strictly defensive. Thus a block of three Powers in the centre of Europe was now united to maintain the peace.

THE THREE EMPERORS' LEAGUE, 1881

A counter-block consisting of Russia and France was the obvious diplomatic reply to the Triple Alliance—and was ultimately constituted (1891). But no such development stood on the cards in 1882, thanks to the ingenuity of Bismarck. The German chancellor had never regarded the alliance with Austria as the last word; it was to be a warning rather than a threat to Russia, and he continued to cherish the hope that the Three Emperors' League might be reconstituted. And matters worked out much as Bismarck desired. The Russians were greatly impressed by the Austro-German alliance, and being involved in various acrimonious disputes with Great Britain in the Near East and Asia, began to see themselves isolated. They thereupon approached Germany for an agreement. Bismarck was delighted, but insisted that it must also include Austria, to which Russia made no objection. The Austrian government, though far from keen, was finally won over after much argument from Bismarck. So the Three Emperors' League was revived by a treaty signed on 18 June, 1881. The most important article (I) read thus:

In case one of the High Contracting Parties should find itself at war with a fourth Great Power, the two others shall maintain towards it a benevolent neutrality, and shall devote their efforts to the localization of the conflict.

This stipulation shall apply likewise to a war between one of the three Powers and Turkey, but only in the case where a previous agreement shall have been reached between the three Courts as to the results of this war.

In the special case where one of them should obtain a more positive support from one of its two Allies, the obligatory value of the present article shall remain in all its force for the third.

In plain language, this meant that Germany and Austria would not assist Great Britain against Russia and that Russia would remain neutral in a Franco-German or Austro-Italian war. It also made it more probable that Russia and Austria would act in harmony, rather than in opposition, in the Near East—as Bismarck always desired. To make this even clearer, other articles of the treaty and a separate protocol stipulated in some detail the policies which Austria and Russia would pursue in the Near East. The secret of this agreement was so rigidly guarded that its very existence was not known for many years, and the first authentic information was published during the World War. Renewed in 1884, it came to an end three years later, in circumstances that will be explained in due course.

THE AUSTRIAN ALLIANCE WITH SERBIA, 1881, AND
WITH RUMANIA, 1883

The Bismarckian system of alliances, which effectively isolated France, was reinforced by two agreements concluded by Austria-Hungary with Balkan
states. In 1881 Austria and Serbia signed a treaty by
which Austria promised to support the reigning dynasty
and to use her influence with the other Powers "to
second the interest of Serbia." In return Serbia promised not to conclude "any political treaty" with another
government without a previous understanding with
Austria and not to tolerate any intrigues against the
Habsburg monarchy, which contained a large number
of subjects of Serbian race.[4] Thus Serbia became an
outpost of Austrian influence in the Balkans. Even
more important was the alliance concluded with Rumania in 1883. Rumania had rendered valuable assistance to Russia in the Turkish war of 1877-78, but
was most ungallantly forced to cede Southern Bes-
sarabia to Russia by the Treaty of Berlin. Rumania
avenged herself by the secret treaty of 30 October,
1883, with Austria-Hungary. Article II ran as follows:

If Rumania, without any provocation on her part, should
be attacked, Austria-Hungary is bound to bring her in
ample time help and assistance against the aggressor. If
Austria-Hungary be attacked in the same circumstances in
a portion of her states bordering on Rumania, the *casus
fœderis* will immediately arise for the latter.

[4] The treaty was renewed, with some modifications, in 1889 and
lasted until 1895.

The phrase "a portion of her states bordering on Rumania" was a euphemism for describing Russia. Germany "adhered" to the treaty immediately, Italy in 1888. The treaty was renewed four times, finally in 1913. With both Serbia and Rumania in her pocket, Austria was seemingly in a strong position to oppose Russian activity in the Balkans in case the Tsar should forget the obligations of the Three Emperors' League.

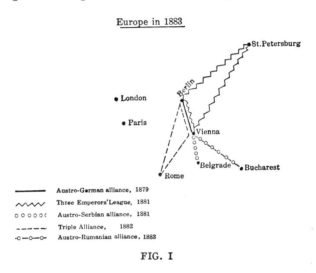

Europe in 1883

————————	Austro-German alliance, 1879
∿∿∿∿	Three Emperors'League, 1881
o o o o o o	Austro-Serbian alliance, 1881
– – – – ~	Triple Alliance, 1882
-o—o—o-	Austro-Rumanian alliance, 1883

FIG. I

GERMAN RELATIONS WITH ENGLAND AND FRANCE

Thus by 1883 an elaborate network of agreements had been wrought in order to fortify the *status quo* in Europe. The situation thus created led to some surprising developments. In the eighteen-eighties the "dark continent" of Africa was being rapidly opened to European penetration. Hitherto Great Britain had been the principal colonizing nation, but now public opinion in Germany vociferously demanded that Germany should acquire outlets for her increasing population and markets for her rapidly expanding trade, and Bismarck, though personally he was not greatly interested, was forced to give heed to this agitation. The German chancellor had managed to maintain fairly cordial and sometimes intimate relations with the British government; in particular he had consistently supported it in the difficult problem of Egypt. He therefore expected the British to show complacency and good-will when Germany embarked upon a policy of colonial expansion. When, to his surprise, he encountered suspicion and opposition, he did not hesitate to show the British how inconvenient and even dangerous it might be to thwart Germany.

As it happened, the French government of the day, under the premiership of Jules Ferry, was pursuing an active colonial policy which created numerous difficulties with Great Britain. Here was Bismarck's opportunity. Though under no illusions as to the intensity of the French desire for *revanche* and the recovery of Alsace-Lorraine, he long cherished the hope that the French might be diverted from the "gap in the Vosges" by the prospect of overseas expansion. "I want to induce you," he said on one occasion to the French ambassador in Berlin, "to pardon Sedan as you have pardoned Waterloo." Indeed, successive French governments after 1875 had pursued such moderate policies that the German chancellor had gladly supported

France in Morocco and encouraged the acquisition of Tunis, which was carried through by the French in 1881. He was accordingly willing to help Ferry against the British, and Ferry was willing to accept this assistance. In 1884-85, then, Europe witnessed the unusual spectacle of France and Germany working in close co-operation against Great Britain in various African questions; Bismarck also supported Ferry in a dispute between France and China over Tonkin.

The real importance of this co-operation lay, however, in the fact that it proved short-lived. The French let Bismarck understand that they were not disposed to renounce Alsace-Lorraine, and without this no permanent friendship would be established. Ferry's policy aroused much resentment in France. Many Frenchmen feared that a trap was being prepared and that France was wasting on colonial ventures energies and resources which should be reserved for a European conflict. When Ferry's policy resulted in a military disaster in Tonkin and he himself incautiously referred to "the precious support of Prince Bismarck," he was overthrown without further ado. The German chancellor was too keen an observer not to appreciate the realities of the situation. Since his tactics had impressed the British with a sense of isolation, not to say a feeling of helplessness, and had induced them to become more tractable on colonial questions, Bismarck in the summer of 1885 made up his quarrel with them. Thus the first attempt to establish a satisfactory relationship between Germany and France had failed.

THE CRISIS IN THE NEAR EAST, 1885-1888

How little the main lines of European politics had been altered by this Franco-German flirtation was exemplified during the long crisis of 1885-88 occasioned by events in the Balkans. In place of the large Bulgaria provided for by the Treaty of San Stefano, the Treaty of Berlin had established a much smaller Bulgaria and had created an autonomous province of Eastern Rumelia within the Turkish Empire. In September, 1885, Eastern Rumelia rose in rebellion against its Turkish governor and proclaimed its union with Bulgaria—which was a direct violation of the Berlin Treaty. It might have been expected that Russia, who had created the "big" Bulgaria and had agreed to the Berlin arrangements very reluctantly, would welcome the revolution which now united the two Bulgarias. But although the Prince of Bulgaria, Alexander of Battenberg, had been appointed by the Russian government, he had refused to do the bidding of Russia in Bulgaria, and the Tsar Alexander III took this as a personal affront. Consequently Russia immediately protested against the union: which was sufficient reason for Great Britain and Austria, who had originally sponsored the division of the big Bulgaria, now to support the union. Germany's attitude was one of reserve, almost of indifference. After long negotiations a compromise was reached whereby the Prince of Bulgaria was appointed governor-general of Eastern Rumelia by the Sultan for a period of five years; by this means the union was effected *de facto,* while nominally the Treaty of Berlin was respected.[5]

There the matter might have ended but for the antagonism of the two Alexanders. As the Bulgarian prince had many enemies among his own people, he was, in August, 1886, kidnapped by some of his own officers and taken to Russia. Though promptly released and allowed to return to Bulgaria, he was forced by Russian pressure to abdicate. The Bulgarian government tried unsuccessfully to find a new prince, but as they refused to submit to Russian dictation, the Tsar finally recalled his representatives and broke off diplomatic relations. Out of this state of affairs there developed a European crisis of the first magnitude.

The Russian attitude towards Bulgaria was deeply resented in Austria-Hungary and Great Britain. Under the pressure of Hungarian opinion, which had been bitterly anti-Russian ever since Russian troops had suppressed the revolutionary movement of 1849, Count Kálnoky, the Austrian foreign minister, was constrained to denounce the Russian action. Austro-Russian relations immediately grew tense, which greatly worried Bismarck: the very situation had now arisen which the Three Emperors' League had been designed to obviate, and Bismarck had to tell the Austrians in blunt language that if they attacked or provoked Rus-

[5] Shortly after the Bulgarian revolution, Serbia, with the connivance of her ally Austria, attacked Bulgaria, on the ground that the Balkan balance of power had been upset by the union of the two Bulgarias. The Serbs were badly defeated and were saved from the vengeance of the victors only by the intervention of Austria. The incident gave the Serbs a bad name politically and a reputation for military incompetence which they were a long time in overcoming.

sia, they would do so at their own risk, for Germany would not consider the treaty of 1879 applicable.

Not only that, but Germany's relations with France were threatening to become difficult. In 1886 a remarkable figure, General Boulanger, had suddenly loomed up in French politics. His speeches and activity marked him out as the apostle of *revanche,* while as minister of war he ostentatiously strengthened the French army in a variety of ways. The government of which he was a member did not desire war, but it might be carried away by the increasing popularity of "le brav' général." At the same time a noisy agitation was getting under way in Russia against the Three Emperors' League, on the ground that it handicapped Russia's action against Austria in the Balkans. Voices were raised in favor of a Franco-Russian alliance, and in the increasing Franco-German tension the Russian government exhibited considerable sympathy for France. Many observers feared that the year 1887 would bring a general European war.

THE MEDITERRANEAN AGREEMENT, 1887

Bismarck dealt with this dangerous situation in masterly fashion. First of all he had passed by the Reichstag a new army bill increasing the strength of the German army—which duly impressed the French. Secondly, he promoted an agreement between Austria, Great Britain and Italy for the maintenance of the *status quo* in the Mediterranean, Adriatic, Ægean and

Black Seas.[6]   By this device he hoped to create a barrier to French and Russian activity without incurring
from Russia the charge of open hostility.   Most important of all, he brought about a change in the Triple
Alliance that was destined to have momentous consequences.   The alliance was due to expire in May, 1887.
The Italian government was ready to renew it—but
not on the old terms.   In spite of his low opinion of
the Italians, Bismarck thought it necessary, in the
existing dangerous situation, to pay their price, and
finally persuaded Kálnoky to do the same.

THE SECOND TREATY OF THE TRIPLE ALLIANCE, 1887

The Triple Alliance of 20 February, 1887, consisted
of three treaties: (1) the old treaty, renewed without
change; (2) a new German-Italian treaty; and (3) a
new Austro-Italian treaty.   Article III of the German-
Italian treaty stipulated that:

If it were to happen that France should make a move to
extend her occupation, or even her protectorate or her sovereignty, under any form whatsoever, in the North African
territories, whether of the Vilayet of Tripoli or of the
Moroccan Empire, and that in consequence thereof Italy,
in order to safeguard her position in the Mediterranean,
should feel that she must herself undertake action in the
said North African territories, or even have recourse to extreme measures in French territories in Europe, the state of
war which would thereby ensue between Italy and France

---

[6] Spain adhered to this agreement, so far as the Mediterranean was
concerned, in May, 1887.

would constitute *ipso facto,* on the demand of Italy and at the common charge of the two Allies, the *casus fœderis.* . . .

According to Article IV:

If the fortunes of war undertaken in common against France should lead Italy to seek for territorial guarantees with respect to France for the security of the frontiers of the Kingdom and of her maritime position, as well as with a view to the stability of peace, Germany will present no obstacle thereto; and, if need be, and in a measure compatible with circumstances, will apply herself to facilitating the means of attaining such a purpose.

Article I of the Austro-Italian treaty bound the two governments to maintain the *status quo* in the Orient "as far as possible," and then continued:

However, if, in the course of events, the maintenance of the *status quo* in the regions of the Balkans or of the Ottoman coasts and islands in the Adriatic and in the Ægean Sea should become impossible, and if, whether in consequence of the action of a third Power or otherwise Austria-Hungary or Italy should find themselves under the necessity of modifying it by a temporary or permanent occupation on their part, this occupation shall take place only after a previous agreement between the two Powers aforesaid, based on the principle of a reciprocal compensation for every advantage, territorial or other, which each of them might obtain beyond the present *status quo,* and giving satisfaction to the interests and well-founded claims of the two Parties.

The first treaty of the Triple Alliance was strictly defensive, but this second edition clearly contemplated changes in the *status quo* for the benefit of two of the three partners. If it was not unreasonable to make provision for changes in the Balkans, the recognition of Italian claims to French territory certainly savored of aggression; the French suspicion that the alliance contained provisions dangerous to them was in fact justified. Remaining true to his dictum that Germany was "saturated," Bismarck claimed no prospective advantage for his own country, but it was none the less a fact that he had been forced to alter the character of the alliance system which he had so laboriously been constructing. The principal article of the Austro-Italian treaty was to prove exceedingly awkward for Germany and Austria in 1914.

THE RUSSO-GERMAN "REINSURANCE" TREATY, 1887

Partly because of the strengthened position of the Central Powers, partly because the troublesome Boulanger was eliminated from the French government in the spring of 1887, war did not break out after all. But the Austro-Russian tension continued so acute that neither government was willing to renew the Three Emperors' League which would expire in June; all efforts of Bismarck to persuade them to divide the Balkans into spheres of influence proved futile. To deal with this situation, the German chancellor needed all his resourcefulness and ingenuity; but he was equal to the occasion. In spite of the dissatisfaction of Pan-Slavist circles, the Russian government was desperately anxious to maintain close relations with Germany, hoping thereby to secure some check on Austria, and it therefore proposed a separate Russo-German treaty to replace the Three Emperors' League. Bismarck accepted the idea with alacrity, and on the day when the Three Emperors' League expired, a new Russo-German secret treaty, the "reinsurance" treaty, as it came to be called, was signed.

The essence of the agreement was contained in Article I, which was drafted by Bismarck himself:

In case one of the High Contracting Parties should find itself at war with a third Great Power, the other would maintain a benevolent neutrality towards it, and would devote its efforts to the localization of the conflict. This provision would not apply to a war against Austria or France in case this war should result from an attack directed against one of these two latter Powers by one of the High Contracting Parties.

Thus Germany was assured of Russian neutrality if she were attacked by France, Russia of German neutrality if she were attacked by Austria or Great Britain. The treaty was not incompatible with the Austro-German alliance of 1879, but certainly a statesman needed Bismarck's iron nerve and cool head to steer a safe course between the demands sure to be made by his Austrian and Russian allies respectively. This is all the more evident when the other provisions of the agreement are considered: Germany recognized "the rights historically acquired by Russia in the Balkan peninsula, and particularly the legitimacy of her preponderant and decisive influence in Bulgaria and in Eastern Rumelia"; Germany promised her assistance to Russia "in order to establish a regular and legal government in Bulgaria," and finally engaged "to ac-

cord her benevolent neutrality and her moral and dip-
lomatic support" to the measures which the Tsar might
deem it necessary to take "to guard the key of his
Empire," i.e., Constantinople. These concessions to
Russia ran counter to policies of Austria and Great
Britain, but Bismarck could make them because the
Mediterranean agreement between Austria, Great
Britain and Italy was strong enough to prevent Russia,
even with the benevolent neutrality of Germany, from
translating them into fact. Bismarck's loyalty towards
Russia has been severely questioned, but his skill in
playing off Russia and her rivals against each other
and thereby consolidating Germany's position against
France was almost uncanny. The reinsurance treaty
remained a deep secret, known only to a few high
officials of the two governments; its very existence was
not even suspected until Bismarck, in 1896, revealed
the fact. Perhaps no other diplomatic episode has been
the theme of more violent controversy.

THE HEIGHT OF THE CRISIS

In July, 1887, the Bulgarians, to the vast indigna-
tion of the Russians, elected a new prince, Ferdinand
of Saxe-Coburg, who was also an officer in the Austrian
army and a Hungarian magnate. Relying upon the
reinsurance treaty, the Russian government appealed
to Germany for assistance in dealing with Bulgaria.
But Bismarck made his support dependent on the
Russians producing a positive programme, and since
they could not or would not do this, the Bulgarian

problem remained unsolved. Russian public opinion blamed Germany for the fiasco, while the Tsar even suspected Bismarck of secretly supporting Prince Ferdinand. Matters became worse when toward the close of the year Russia began to increase her armaments along the German and Austrian frontiers. The German and Austrian general staffs urged a preventive war. Once more the war clouds seemed to be gathering.

The German chancellor dissipated them with a few masterly strokes. The Russian government had long been accustomed to borrow in the German money market, and large quantities of its securities were held in Germany. In November, 1887, Bismarck ordered that henceforth Russian securities should no longer be accepted as collateral, which effectively prevented the flotation of further Russian loans in Germany. The measure came at a difficult moment for the Russian state finances and acted as a brake on Russian policy. To that extent it achieved its immediate purpose. In the long run, however, the consequences were not so happy. For not only was Russian opinion more hostile to Germany than ever, but the Russian government was forced henceforth to borrow in Paris—and the close financial relations thus established proved an all-important factor in the establishment of the Franco-Russian alliance.

On the political side, Bismarck cordially approved an Italian proposal that the Mediterranean agreement of February, 1887, should be extended and strengthened, which was accomplished in December.[7] Though refusing to accept the soldiers' demand for a preventive war, he urged Austria-Hungary to increase her armaments and laid before the German Reichstag a supplementary army bill. Most striking of all, he published the text of the Austro-German alliance of 1879, which made clear to the excited Russians that an attack on Austria would also involve war with Germany. In a famous speech delivered a few days later Bismarck declared that Germany was able to fight a war on two fronts: "We Germans fear God and nothing else in the world," were his ringing words. Realizing its helplessness, the Russian government washed its hands of Bulgaria, while in France the moderates united to get rid of General Boulanger. By the spring of 1888 the tension of the winter had largely disappeared. Bismarck's complicated system of alliances and agreements had justified itself.

BISMARCK'S OVERTURE TO ENGLAND, 1889

But Russo-German relations did not revive their former cordiality, Pan-Slavic opinion remaining openly hostile and the official attitude somewhat suspicious. Russia, indeed, at this time arranged to purchase large quantities of the new Lebel rifle which had just been perfected in France. Bismarck now took the obvious

[7] Whereas the original agreement was merely a diplomatic understanding, Austria, Great Britain and Italy now agreed to reach an understanding, if necessary, as to the measures "for causing to be respected the independence of the Ottoman Empire and the integrity of its territory, as secured by previous treaties."

step of once more approaching Great Britain with the
suggestion of an alliance directed primarily against
France. Lord Salisbury, the British prime minister,
professed to be personally favorable to the idea, but
declared that parliament would reject any formal com-
mitment and therefore declined the proposal. Bismarck realized that the reinsurance treaty had lost
much of its value, but it was better than nothing, and
in view of the British refusal, he deemed it essential
to secure the renewal of the treaty, which would expire
in June, 1890. The Tsar, though disappointed with the
results of the treaty, was willing, for he did not wish
Russia to be isolated. Accordingly in March, 1890,
negotiations were begun for the renewal.

BISMARCK'S FALL: LAPSE OF THE REINSURANCE
TREATY, 1890

But by this time Bismarck's position had become
hopelessly compromised. He had always been able,
albeit at times with difficulty, to manipulate the old
Emperor William I and pursue his own policy. Frederick III, who succeeded his father in 1888, had long
been on bad terms with the chancellor, but he was a
dying man and lived only three months. It was with
the accession of William II in June, 1888, that Bismarck's troubles began. The young Emperor was an
enthusiastic admirer of the great chancellor, but he
quickly came to resent the domination of Bismarck.
Gradually many differences of opinion manifested
themselves between the two men, more particularly

on matters of internal politics, but sometimes also in the realm of foreign policy. Bismarck's many enemies in Germany did their best to widen the breach. Hardly had the negotiations with Russia begun when the quarrel between William II and Bismarck came to a head, and the chancellor was dismissed. The Emperor had given his consent to the renewal of the treaty, but the Russian government now refused to continue the negotiations until the new chancellor was appointed. As it happened, the principal personage in the German foreign office—after Bismarck—Friedrich von Holstein, had long opposed the Russian treaty, believing that it was incompatible with the Austrian alliance. Holstein was also a bitter personal enemy of Bismarck. He therefore took advantage of the situation to persuade the new chancellor, General von Caprivi, an honest soldier with no experience in diplomacy, that the reinsurance treaty should not be renewed. Caprivi may well have believed that, as he said, the Bismarckian system of alliances was "too complicated," and it may be that only Bismarck could have operated it successfully.

Nevertheless, the failure to renew the treaty was probably a blunder. The Russian foreign minister, Giers, plead eloquently and frequently for the conclusion of some kind of agreement. Both he and the Tsar disliked the prospect of isolation and were very reluctant to make an alliance with France; they were therefore anxious, in spite of Russian public opinion, to maintain the connection with Germany. It was precisely because he understood this that Bismarck attached so much importance to the treaty: so long as it existed, Russia would not seek the alliance of France. Perhaps Bismarck was at fault in not having made sufficiently clear to the Emperor the intricate system of checks and balances by which he had managed for twenty years to maintain Germany's position unchallenged in the centre of Europe, but it would seem as if his system was discarded chiefly because it was his and not on any deep appreciation of its merits.

Whether the action of the German government was wise or not—and it is a much-disputed question among historians—the passing of Bismarck marked the end of an epoch. German policy passed under the control of new men without experience, while elsewhere in Europe there were no statesmen who possssed his resourcefulness or daring.

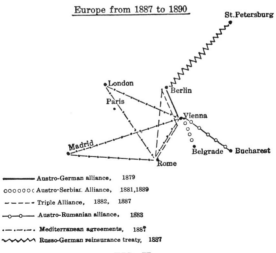

Europe from 1887 to 1890

St.Petersburg
London
Berlin
Paris
Vienna
Madrid
Belgrade   Bucharest
Rome

———————— Austro-German alliance, 1879
oooooo(Austro-Serbian Alliance, 1881,1889
– – – – – Triple Alliance, 1882, 1887
—o——o— Austro-Rumanian alliance, 1883
.—.—.—. Mediterranean agreements, 1887
⋀⋀⋀⋀ Russo-German reinsurance treaty, 1887

FIG. II

II

THE TRIPLE ENTENTE

HAVING broken the "wire to St. Petersburg" the German government did what Bismarck would have done: it concluded an agreement with Great Britain (July, 1890) by which the latter ceded Heligoland to Germany in return for territory in Africa. But neither this move nor the manifestation of a less friendly German policy towards Russia in the Near East sufficed to bring Russia much closer to France. For years the Russians had understood that in the event of war with Germany they could count upon the French: for which reason they had always seen to it that France was not treated too roughly by Germany. But beyond this they were not anxious to go, as was revealed by an incident early in 1891. The Empress Frederick, mother of William II, had unwisely paid a visit to Paris, where she acted somewhat indiscreetly. When popular manifestations forced her to leave Paris, rumors of German mobilization and impending war began to fly about. The French government inquired what the Russian attitude would be, and received an evasive answer.

Nevertheless a few months later a diplomatic agreement was concluded between France and Russia. For several years the French government had been zealously trying to detach Italy from the Triple Alliance, using a variety of means: promises of favors in Africa, a tariff war, support of papal pretensions for the recovery of the temporal power, and even bribery. But all to no avail. Italy felt herself so dependent on Great Britain that, in spite of the unpopularity of the Triple Alliance in many quarters, she was unwilling, at a moment when Anglo-French relations were exceedingly strained on account of Egypt, to exchange British for French friendship. Moreover, the Italian government had succeeded in securing an important extension of the Triple Alliance when it was renewed in May, 1891. Not only were the three treaties of 1887 combined in a single instrument, but a new article was added, as follows:

Article IX. Germany and Italy engage to exert themselves for the maintenance of the territorial *status quo* in the North African regions on the Mediterranean, to wit, Cyrenaica, Tripolitania and Tunisia. . . .

If unfortunately, as a result of a mature examination of the situation, Germany and Italy should both recognize that the maintenance of the *status quo* has become impossible, Germany engages, after a formal and previous agreement, to support Italy in any action in the form of occupation or other taking of guarantee which the latter should undertake in these same regions with a view to an interest of equilibrium and of legitimate compensation.

It is understood that in such an eventuality the two Powers would seek to place themselves likewise in agreement with England.

The renewal of the alliance was announced in the early summer of 1891 with a good deal of noise. Furthermore a debate in the British parliament elicited the statement from the government that while Great Britain was not a member of the Triple Alliance, it was disposed to co-operate with the alliance, and especially with Italy, for the maintenance of the *status quo* in the Mediterranean and Near East. By way of reinforcing this declaration, a British fleet visited Austrian and Italian waters. Also the German Emperor visited London and was enthusiastically received. It was this general situation which finally drew Russia and France, both of them isolated and fearing that Great Britain might join the Triple Alliance, into a diplomatic understanding. Even so, the Russians appear to have been somewhat reluctant, but a French hint that future loans were dependent on a bargain brought them to terms.

THE FRANCO-RUSSIAN ALLIANCE, 1891-1894

A preliminary step was taken by a French fleet visiting Cronstadt, the Russian naval base near St. Petersburg. All Europe was properly shocked when the autocratic Tsar listened bareheaded to the playing of the *Marseillaise,* but there was no doubt about the Franco-Russian partnership. This was formally consecrated by an exchange of notes between the two governments on 27 August, 1891, which read as follows:

1. In order to define and consecrate the cordial understanding which unites them, and in their desire to contribute with one accord to the maintenance of peace, which is the

object of their sincerest wishes, the two governments declare that they will confer on every question of a nature to threaten the general peace.

2. In case this peace should actually be in danger, and especially in case one of the two parties should be threatened by aggression, the two parties agree to come to an understanding on the measures which the realization of that eventuality would make it necessary for both governments to adopt immediately and simultaneously.

This vague and somewhat limited agreement enabled France and Russia to present a united diplomatic front, particularly against Great Britain. But it contained no military guarantees analogous to those of the Austro-German and Triple Alliances, and the French were not satisfied with mere assurances of Russian good-will. They could never rid themselves of the fear that they might be attacked by Germany, particularly as the German Emperor, by virtue of bellicose speeches and other theatrical performances, was regarded as an unstable factor. The French government accordingly began to press for a military convention, and in 1892 an understanding was reached between the French and Russian general staffs. The French wished Russia to devote her principal attention to Germany, whereas the Russians not unnaturally regarded Austria as their principal enemy; in the end, a compromise was adopted.

The Tsar Alexander III, however, long refused to ratify the convention. Both he and Giers still hoped for some kind of understanding with Germany, which showed a willingness to make a favorable commercial treaty. Moreover, the Tsar did not intend that Russia should be drawn into a war with Germany by a French policy of *revanche*. Two events finally turned the scales. In the first place, a new German army bill of 1893, while it reduced the term of service from three to two years, increased the peace strength of the German army. Secondly, during this same year while Russia was advancing against the Pamirs in central Asia, to the annoyance of Great Britain, France made a determined stand against the British in Siam. The French attitude was so threatening that war seemed likely and the British government appealed to Germany for help. This apparently convinced the Tsar that France would be a welcome ally against Great Britain and that her policy towards Germany was pacific. Accordingly he gave his consent to the ratification of the military convention, which went into effect in January, 1894.

Like the other alliances and agreements, the terms of the Franco-Russian convention were kept rigidly secret, the terms not being published until 1918, when the alliance had been dissolved under the stress of the World War. The essential provisions were:

Article 1. If France is attacked by Germany, or by Italy supported by Germany, Russia shall employ all her available forces to fight Germany [fixed in a subsequent article at "from 700,000 to 800,000 men"].

If Russia is attacked by Germany, or by Austria supported by Germany, France shall employ all her available forces to fight Germany [fixed in a subsequent article at 1,300,000 men].

Article 2. In case the forces of the Triple Alliance or one of the Powers which compose it should be mobilized,

France and Russia, at the first indication of the event, and without a previous agreement being necessary, shall mobilize all their forces immediately and simultaneously, and shall transport them as near to the frontiers as possible. [This article is explained by the agreement of the French and Russian general staffs that "mobilization means war."]

It was further agreed that the two countries should not conclude peace separately and that the convention should have the same duration as the Triple Alliance.[1]

It will be noted that although the circumstances which induced the conclusion of the diplomatic agreement and the ratification of the military convention lay largely outside of Europe, yet the provisions of the alliance related to the European situation. This was inevitable, for clashes between the Powers on account of extra-European interests would, in the last analysis, have to be fought out in Europe. But while special circumstances brought the Franco-Russian alliance into existence in 1891-94, probably such a consummation was bound to come sooner or later. A Bismarck might succeed in making the French connection unnecessary to Russia, while the French shied at the idea so long as the internal situation of their country was unsettled and obscure. But Bismarck could not last forever, and after 1890 the Republican régime in France was so firmly established that the government could and did consider a more active foreign policy. Certainly the existence of a strong alliance in the centre

---

[1] In 1899 it was agreed that the convention should remain in force as long as the diplomatic agreement of 1891, in which there was interpolated an understanding to maintain "the European balance of power."

of Europe, no matter how pacific its intentions—and the peaceful professions of the Triple Alliance were not always believed—called for the establishment of a counterweight if the balance of power was to be preserved. And in fact, the creation of the Franco-Russian alliance, the existence of which was publicly admitted in 1895, established such a balance of military power that for the next ten years Europe was spared crises like those of 1875, 1878, 1885-88. Troubled moments there were, but they arose out of overseas rivalries of the Powers, not from threats to the European equilibrium or from disturbances in the ever-restless Balkans. The Dual Alliance and the Triple Alliance did, it would seem, guarantee the peace of Europe; at least they preserved it. During these years the two groups stood side by side; often there was considerable co-operation between them. Only later developments caused them to take position face to face.

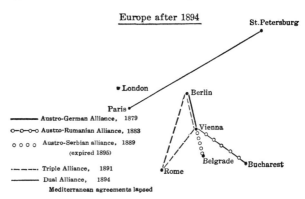

FIG. III

THE ALLIANCES AND THE EXPANSION OF EUROPE

Since the most immediate consequence of the Franco-Russian alliance was to give stability to the European situation, it is not surprising that the tendencies towards expansion overseas which had been manifesting themselves before 1894 should have been even more in evidence after that date. For the next ten years the primary interests of European governments seemed to be found, not in the Near East (although a serious crisis arose there in the middle of the 'nineties), but in various parts of Africa and in the Far East. If the old considerations of the balance of power were not lost sight of, the relations between governments tended to be affected much more by their rivalries in Africa and Asia than by the traditional motives of strictly European politics. International relations entered upon a period of flux in which the continued existence of the Triple and Dual Alliances in no way prevented the formation of temporary combinations of powers for particular ends. In general the assumption seems to have been that if the undeveloped regions of the world and the boundless opportunities for concessions could be more or less reasonably divided among the Great Powers, the European situation would take care of itself. It was only after the turn of the century that the reactions of these world-wide rivalries began to be felt by European politics in the strict sense, and it was not until 1905 that the centre of gravity in international relations was discovered once more to be in Europe.

The coincidence that the year 1894 was marked not only by the ratification of the Franco-Russian alliance but also by a considerable change in the personnel of European statesmen doubtless contributed to the universal enthusiasm for overseas expansion. In France Gabriel Hanotaux, who believed firmly in the colonial policy of Jules Ferry, became minister of foreign affairs and held the office during most of the time until 1898. In Germany the cautious General von Caprivi was replaced as chancellor by Prince Hohenlohe, a statesman of advanced years who could not or did not exert much control over the foreign office. The Tsar Alexander III, a staunch supporter of peace and an opponent of adventures, died; his son and successor, Nicholas II, was a weak character who left Russian diplomacy a free hand. In Great Britain the old Liberal prime minister, W. E. Gladstone, who was constantly accused of indifference to the interests of the British Empire, retired from office in favor of Lord Rosebery, who was a convinced imperialist; in the following year the Liberals gave way to the Conservatives, whose leader, Lord Salisbury, was always responsive to the call of empire. The new leaders did not invent policies of expansion and imperialism, but they applied them with a vigor and to an extent that was not possible in the 'eighties. In the scramble which followed, countries which were rivals in Europe might find their interests more or less identical beyond the seas, while Powers which had worked in harmony in Europe might fall out in Africa or Asia.

In the ten years from 1894 to 1904, three main

tendencies can be discerned in international politics. First of all, Russia very largely abandoned Europe and became absorbed in the Far East. When fearful massacres occurred in Armenia in 1894-96, Russia, instead of exploiting the opportunity to realize her traditional ambitions, gave at first only luke-warm support to Great Britain, who wished to impose serious reforms on Turkey, and then openly espoused the side of the Sultan; with the result, of course, that nothing was done. How anxious Russia was to prevent a reopening of the Eastern question was shown by the agreement made in 1897 with Austria-Hungary, her ancient rival, to maintain the *status quo* and to restrain the Balkan states.

Thus protected, Russia plunged ahead in the Far East. When in 1895, Japan, having defeated China in war, compelled the latter to cede, among other possessions, the Liaotung peninsula and the harbor of Port Arthur, the Russian government, with the support of France and Germany, intervened and forced Japan to surrender her gains to China. A few years later Russia seized Port Arthur for herself, then proceeded, during the Boxer uprising, to occupy Manchuria, and ultimately became involved in war with Japan (1904). This absorption of Russia in Far Eastern problems was very welcome to Germany and enthusiastically encouraged by her. It permitted Germany to acquire Far Eastern interests of her own (occupation of Kiao-Chow and lease of Shantung, 1898) and relieved her of all danger of a war on two fronts. From the point of

view of strictly European politics, the Dual Alliance
had become a broken reed.

The second tendency of these years was the so-called
policy of the "free hand" adopted by Germany. The
alliance of France and Russia might become very dangerous to Germany, but Germany was able to trade on
the fact that France and Russia were, in the 'nineties,
both on bad terms with Great Britain, France in Africa
and Russia in Asia. The German foreign office endeavored therefore, more particularly after 1897 when
Bernhard von Bülow became foreign minister, to play
France and Russia off against Great Britain, siding now
with one and then with the other, and seeking always
to secure something for Germany. Thus, in 1894,
when the British and Belgian governments concluded
a treaty providing for the exchange of certain territories bordering on the Congo Free State, of which
the King of the Belgians was the sovereign, Germany
promptly joined with France in protesting that their
rights were affected, and the treaty had to be abandoned. In the following year, Germany assisted Russia
and France in compelling Japan to disgorge part of the
spoils of her war with China, thus, as it were, neutral-
izing the Dual Alliance in Europe by converting it into
a Far Eastern Triple Alliance. And even greater possibilities seemed to open up.

In the last days of 1895 the long-simmering dispute
between the British and the Boers in South Africa
came to a head in the Jameson raid. The German
government had already given encouragement to the
Boers, and now the German Emperor took it upon him-

self to send a telegram of congratulation to President Krüger of the Transvaal (3 January, 1896). In addition the German foreign office sounded France on the possibility of co-operation in order to prevent the continuous expansion of the British Empire, and even made an overture to Russia. The idea clearly was to bring about some kind of continental coalition against Great Britain. It was not the last time that Germany was to come forward with this suggestion.

But the plan was coldly received in both Paris and St. Petersburg (the French are said to have revealed it to London), and Germany soon shifted her policy. By way of appeasing the British for some two years of pretty constant opposition, she now supported the proposal of the Egyptian government, i.e., the British, which was opposed by France and Russia, that certain surplus funds under international control should be used for an expedition to conquer the Sudan. The expedition was indeed desired in Berlin in order to relieve the pressure on Germany's ally, Italy, whose attempt to conquer Abyssinia had been brought to an inglorious end by a stinging defeat at Adowa by Abyssinian troops. By 1898 the German government had reached the conclusion that its anti-British policy was yielding small results and that the time had come for a rapprochement with Great Britain.

What happened in consequence of this decision is to be explained by the third main tendency of the 'nineties, namely, the growing isolation of Great Britain. Isolation was indeed the favorite policy of Great Britain, but Salisbury had felt compelled to abandon it in 1887 to the extent of concluding the Mediterranean agreements with Italy (see above, pp. 27-28). As late as 1891 he was co-operating closely with the Triple Alliance and thereby helped bring France and Russia together (see above, pp. 39-40). But when the Near Eastern question ceased to be dangerous the agreements were allowed to lapse, and when Salisbury returned to office in 1895 he went so far as to suggest to the German Emperor the desirability of partitioning the Ottoman Empire among the interested Powers. Although this had been consistently advocated by Bismarck—and rejected by England—it was now regarded with great suspicion by William II and his government and promptly turned down. The British for their part greatly resented the German interference in Africa (Congo, Transvaal). Yet their controversy with France over Egypt was becoming steadily more intense, while Russia's activity in China was causing increasing alarm. In short, Great Britain in 1898 was well-nigh isolated in Europe. It was not without significance that when the Spanish-American war broke out the continental powers all sympathized with Spain and favored an attempt at mediation. Only Great Britain supported the United States.

In spite of the immense superiority of the British fleet to all others, there was a limit to the number of enemies. The ever-realistic Salisbury therefore approached the Russian government with the suggestion of a rapprochement. At first Count Lamsdorff, the Russian foreign minister, was friendly, and so was Witte, the all-powerful minister of finance. But this did not last long. Perhaps the Russians calculated that the British were too weak to oppose serious opposition to their ambitions in the Far East. At any rate the negotiations were soon broken off. Since the French were in no need for concessions in Egypt, Germany remained the only possible partner for Great Britain. Thus British and German moods in 1898 harmonized to the extent of desiring to reach an understanding.

THE BRITISH CHANGE OF FRONT: NEGOTIATIONS FOR AN ANGLO-GERMAN ALLIANCE, 1898-1901

So in March, 1898, Joseph Chamberlain, the British colonial secretary, made overtures to the German ambassador in London for an Anglo-German alliance, which would be ratified by the British parliament in order to ensure its observance by subsequent cabinets. Bülow professed to fear that parliament would not ratify the treaty because of resentment over the Krüger telegram, and allowed the proposal to evaporate.[2] During the summer, however, when Portugal was reported to be in financial straits, Great Britain and Germany signed a convention by which they agreed to consult as to the terms of any loans which might be made to Portugal and to divide the Portuguese colonies, the tolls of which might be pledged as security for the

[2] The German Emperor, with a complete lack of honesty, informed the Tsar that England had made him a very attractive offer, and asked for a Russian counter-offer. Nicholas II replied that England had previously made overtures to Russia, and that William must decide what was best for Germany.

loans. Actually Portugal was not in desperate circumstances and made loans which did not involve
pledging the colonial customs. And not only did the
contingent partition not materialize, but in October,
1899, Great Britain and Portugal renewed their ancient alliance by which Great Britain undertook to
defend the Portuguese colonies.

In spite of these first failures, the British government did not give up hope of an alliance with Germany.
When William II came to England in the autumn of
1899, Chamberlain and Bülow once more discussed
the possibilities. The German minister appeared so
favorable to an alliance that Chamberlain broached it
publicly in a famous speech at Leicester. Bülow, however, poured cold water on the idea in a speech to the
Reichstag. It is true that other members of the British
cabinet were by no means so enthusiastic for an alliance as Chamberlain, but Bülow's conduct was much
resented in England. The German government did not
improve matters by raising in rather acrimonious
fashion an old controversy about Samoa and insisting
on a settlement to which Great Britain would hardly
have agreed had she not been involved in the Boer
War.

German opinion sympathized strongly with the Boers
and expressed itself in violent terms. It was further
irritated when the British seized some German ships
in South African waters. These incidents greatly facil-
itated the passage by the Reichstag of a navy law
which provided for the construction of a formidable
fleet by 1920, a fleet so strong, according to the official

explanation, that "even for the adversary with the greatest sea power a war against it would involve such dangers as to imperil his own position in the world."

Fortunately the two governments kept their heads. Germany declined Russian proposals for intervention at London to help the Boers, and in October, 1900, an Anglo-German agreement was signed to respect and maintain the integrity of China. William II's journey to London at the death of Queen Victoria (January, 1901) was much appreciated in England. So shortly afterwards formal negotiations were begun for an alliance—on whose initiative is not clear. Germany agreed in principle, but insisted that Great Britain should join the Triple Alliance, for, she argued, an alliance would involve her in war with Russia. Salisbusy was not keen for any kind of alliance, but allowed Lansdowne, who had become foreign secretary, to see what he could do; Lansdowne, for his part, was unwilling to assume responsibility for Austria-Hungary, whose condition was far from reassuring. So the negotiations ran into the sand. An attempt made during the summer to reach some understanding about Morocco also came to naught. Curiously enough, Germany had also suggested the inclusion of Japan in the alliance. The British were willing, and, although the negotiations with Germany failed, an Anglo-Japanese alliance was concluded in January, 1902. This marked the first formal departure by Great Britain from her traditional isolation.

Since the World War, the refusal of Germany to accept any of the several overtures for an alliance has been sharply criticized by many German historians. Had such an agreement been consummated, the history of the world might well have been different, for the strongest naval and the strongest military power would have been united to preserve the peace. But it may be doubted whether the alliance would have been long harmonious unless Germany had been willing to rely on the British fleet and renounce her own naval ambitions—which was very far from the intentions of William II and his stalwart minister of the navy, Admiral von Tirpitz. In the negotiations Bülow always emphasized the danger to Germany from the inevitable hostility of Russia, who would be joined by France in the event of war. But the real German motives for declining the British alliance were deeper. Bülow believed, in the first place, that Germany was strong enough to play a lone hand. He assured William II that he was the "arbiter mundi" and later asserted that the Triple Alliance was not "an absolute necessity." The Emperor for his part declared that the balance of power in Europe rested upon "me and my twenty-five army corps." In the second place, Bülow and Holstein, at heart, desired an alliance with Great Britain—but on their own terms. They had convinced themselves that Britain's differences with France and Russia were so deep-rooted that, in spite of warnings from Chamberlain, no accommodation was possible. Britain, they argued, could never pay the price which France and Russia would demand for an understanding; therefore, in the end, Germany could exact her own price.

Unfortunately, Bülow and Holstein guessed wrong. For the British, having failed utterly to reach an agreement with Germany, did exactly what Chamberlain had said they would do—they turned to France. Although Great Britain was a stronger power than Germany, her statesmen had become keenly conscious of the dangers of isolation and they determined to find friends for their country.

FASHODA, 1898

An Anglo-French rapprochement was made possible by two circumstances. In the first place, the most serious difficulty between the two countries had been, in effect, liquidated before the end of the century. In 1896, when France and Russia had refused to allow certain surplus Egyptian funds to be used for the reconquest of the Sudan (see above, p. 49), the British government had found the necessary money and despatched an expedition under Sir Herbert Kitchener to do the job. Kitchener had hardly defeated the native army of the Sudan at the battle of Omdurman, near Khartum (September, 1898), when he learned that a French expedition under Major Marchand had arrived at Fashoda some five hundred miles to the south. This expedition had been sent out by the French government from its territories in West Africa in the hope of anticipating the British in the Sudan, and it actually reached Fashoda in July. Kitchener proceeded from Khartum to Fashoda and invited Marchand to retire, which he declined to do;

the two commanders thereupon referred the question to their governments.

It was a vital decision for France, for the British government politely but firmly made clear that it would fight rather than recognize any French claim to the Sudan. France was not in a position to take up the challenge. Her fleet was inferior to the British; her ally Russia was busy in the Far East and reluctant to act in Europe; Germany had recently signed with Great Britain the convention concerning the Portuguese colonies. As it happened, the Anglophobe Hanotaux had ceased to be minister of foreign affairs a few months before the crisis broke. His successor, Théophile Delcassé, although he argued the French case manfully and ingeniously with Salisbury, could only agree to withdraw Marchand's force when the British insisted. Once this had been settled, Salisbury made the surrender easier by recognizing a strip of Eastern Sahara as falling within the French sphere of influence (Bahr-el-Gazal), which gave France a commercial outlet to the valley of the Nile. This agreement, recorded in a convention of 20 March, 1899, really settled the long-standing Egyptian question in favor of Great Britain. To be sure, the French government did not formally recognize the British "occupation," and there remained many other disputes between France and Great Britain in various parts of the world. But the fundamental obstacle to an agreement, when the passions of the moment subsided, was removed.

The second circumstance favoring an Anglo-French rapprochement was the new orientation being given to French policy by Delcassé. He perceived that the diplomatic position of France was weak so long as she relied solely on Russia, for Germany, in spite of her many overtures for co-operation, was no more liked or trusted than she had been in the 'seventies and 'eighties. Moreover, in Delcassé's mind, Germany was the "hereditary enemy," no matter how much France might quarrel with England overseas. So he assumed office with the determination to liquidate France's difficulties with Great Britain and Italy and thus recover for her a large measure of diplomatic freedom. The Egyptian question being disposed of for the time being by the Convention of 1899, Delcassé turned his attention to Italy.

FRANCE AND ITALY, 1898-1902

The relations between the two "Latin sisters" had been strained for years. France always regarded the Triple Alliance with suspicion, and not without reason, for although the terms of the alliance were not known, they were dangerous to France. As long as Crispi, a bitter Francophobe, was in power in Italy, the ill-feeling that dated from the French occupation of Tunis had no chance of dying down, and it was stimulated by a long tariff war between the two countries. But after the disaster at Adowa, Crispi fell, and his successors became anxious for a rapprochement with France. The tariff war was brought to an end in 1898, and the economic situation in Italy immediately improved. Thus the way was paved for a political agreement in 1900, by which France and Italy recognized each other's aspirations in Morocco and Tripoli respectively. If the French hoped to detach Italy from the Triple Alliance, they were disappointed, for in 1902 that instrument was renewed for a period of twelve years. But the Italian foreign minister, Prinetti, a pronounced Francophile, declared that the alliance had been renewed without change and allowed Delcassé to publish the assurance that it contained nothing either directly or indirectly directed against France. This was followed by a secret agreement on 1 November, 1902, to the following effect:

> In case France [Italy] should be the object of a direct or indirect aggression on the part of one or more powers, Italy [France] will maintain a strict neutrality.
>
> The same shall hold good in case France [Italy], as the result of a direct provocation, should find herself compelled, in defense of her honor or her security, to take the initiative of a declaration of war.

The real meaning of this bargain was that if France, in consequence of her alliance with Russia, should declare war on Germany, Italy would not go to the assistance of Germany. It was not contrary to the *letter* of the Triple Alliance, but it assuredly was, as a French writer has recognized, "hard to reconcile" with its spirit. The German government was aware that something was going on between Italy and France, but tried to discount it. Bülow, in his airy way, asserted that in a happy marriage the husband did not mind if his wife indulged in an innocent "extra dance." German calculations were, however, henceforth based on the assumption that Italy was not to be relied on, and this

proved to be the case. The new Franco-Italian harmony was signalled to the world by an interchange of
visits between President Loubet and King Victor Em-
manuel. His mind free about the Mediterranean, Delcassé was in a position to try effectively for a real
rapprochement with Great Britain.

THE *ENTENTE CORDIALE,* 1904

The first decisive step came, however, from the
British side. In 1903 King Edward VII decided to
pay a state visit to the President of the French Republic. The King was as strongly French in his sympathies as his mother had been German, and as Prince
of Wales he had always been highly popular with the
Parisians. He relied on this fact and on his own personality to break down what ill-feeling toward Britain
there still remained in France after Fashoda and the
Boer War. His visit abundantly justified itself, for
although on the first day he was coldly received he was
being cheered before he left. A few months later
President Loubet returned the visit, and on this occasion the two foreign ministers, Lansdowne and Delcassé, opened negotiations. They were long and difficult, but on both sides there was a determination to
succeed. The matter was brought to a head by the
Russo-Japanese war which broke out in February
1904. Since France was the ally of one belligerent
and Great Britain of the other, it was obvious that an
understanding would remove any danger of their both
being drawn into the war.

The agreement of 8 April, 1904, consisted of three documents. The first was a convention which settled the old question of the Newfoundland fisheries, modified certain boundaries between French and British colonies in Africa, and gave the Iles de Los to France. The second was a declaration by which old quarrels over Siam, Madagascar and the New Hebrides were adjusted. The third and by far the most important dealt with Egypt and Morocco. By the terms of this declaration France relinquished her rights and interests in Egypt in favor of Great Britain, and Great Britain hers in Morocco in favor of France. The open door was guaranteed for thirty years, the rights of Spain in Morocco were to be respected, and the south shore of the Straits of Gibraltar was not to be fortified. By Article IX

the two governments agree to afford to one another their diplomatic support, in order to obtain the execution of the clauses of the present declaration regarding Egypt and Morocco.

The published declaration pledged the two Powers to maintain the *status quo* in Egypt and Morocco; but in secret articles, not published till 1911, provision was made for an eventual partition of Morocco between France and Spain. This secret agreement was much criticized when it became known, but there was much to be said for arranging the details of partition quietly and before the issue arose.

The accord, or the *Entente cordiale* as it soon came to be known, was very favorably received in

Great Britain except by a few "die-hards." In France the attitude was more mixed, and the Anglophobes had a field day in the Chamber of Deputies, the argument being that France was surrendering in Egypt much more than Great Britain in Morocco. But reason prevailed, the accord was ratified—and a new diplomatic constellation had appeared in the European diplomatic sky.

So far as the written word went, the Anglo-French *entente* merely effected a liquidation of difficulties beyond the sea. Europe was nowhere mentioned. Yet Europe was inevitably and profoundly affected, and beyond a doubt this was in the back of the minds of the experienced diplomatists who negotiated the agreement. So long as Great Britain and France wrangled about territories and claims in Asia and Africa, they exposed themselves to the fine touch of Bülow and Holstein, who played one off against the other and demanded "compensation" for the services which Germany claimed to be rendering. This was no longer possible. Since Great Britain and France were pledged to diplomatic cooperation in Egypt and Morocco, it was unlikely that they would fail to cooperate in other fields if necessity arose. In 1904 their agreement was no more than what it pretended to be—a settlement of colonial rivalries. It was not *per se* directed against Germany, but it did impose a barrier to the German policy of the "free hand." The future of Anglo-French relations depended on German reaction to the *Entente cordiale*, and that story is best reserved for the next chapter.

THE ANGLO-RUSSIAN AGREEMENT, 1907

The situation resulting from the Anglo-French agreement was anomalous in the sense that France, the ally
of Russia, was now on cordial terms with Great
Britain, the ally of Japan who was at war with Russia.
Delcassé was determined to complete the diplomatic
structure he was building by promoting an understanding between Great Britain and Russia, and made no
secret of it. The British were equally willing. Lansdowne had in fact made overtures to Russia in 1903,
but nothing came of it because the Russians believed
Great Britain to be inciting Japan. In the following
year King Edward discreetly sounded the Russian
minister in Copenhagen, but again without result.
Events were, however, moving, almost inexorably one
might say, to bring about Anglo-Russian negotiations.
The defeat of Russia in the Far East by Japan threw
the great Slav Power back on Europe, back on the
Near East which had been neglected for so many years.
There Russia found a situation quite different from
that of twenty years before. Then it was Great Britain
who constantly opposed Russian policy towards Turkey, while Germany either stood aloof or secretly encouraged Russia. But by 1905 Germany had come
forward as the champion of Turkey, seeking to re-
juvenate it economically by the Bagdad Railway and
supporting Sultan Abdul-Hamid whose tyrannical rule
in Macedonia was so harshly felt by Russia's Slavic
kinsmen. Great Britain, on the other hand, had, since
the days of the Armenian massacres, turned more and

more against Turkey, and being established in Egypt, was more indifferent to her fate than hitherto.

Within Russia the revolution of 1905 and the establishment of the Duma in 1906 gave some chance to Russian liberalism and helped prepare the atmosphere for an agreement with liberal England. True, the Russian conservatives were hostile, but the foreign minister, A. P. Izvolsky, who had succeeded Lamsdorff on the latter's death, was a liberal who sincerely desired closer and friendlier relations with England. Moreover, Izvolsky had been a consistent opponent of the Far Eastern adventure and believed that Russia's mission lay in Europe. But if a Near Eastern policy was to be successfully pursued, quarrels elsewhere with Great Britain would have to be adjusted, even at the price of large concessions.

In Great Britain the advent of the Liberal party to power in December 1905 augured well. Sir Edward Grey, the new foreign secretary, had not only welcomed the *entente* with France before he took office, but he had declared that an understanding with Russia was also desirable. If any further incentive were needed, it was provided by the dramatic events of 1905-1906 which will be set forth in the next chapter.

The negotiations between Great Britain and Russia, begun in the spring of 1906, dragged along for more than a year. Izvolsky had a good deal of trouble with conservative and military elements who were traditionally suspicious of Great Britain. Grey for his part, very ably advised by his ambassador in St. Petersburg, Sir Arthur Nicolson, exhibited the utmost patience and yielded gracefully when he could not gain a point. The agreement of 31 August, 1907, consisted of three documents dealing with Tibet, Afghanistan and Persia, the most important provision being the division of Persia into three spheres of influence, one Russian in the north, a second British in the south, and the third neutral lying between the other two. In addition Great Britain reaffirmed her position in the Persian Gulf. Analyzed in detail, the settlement was more advantageous to Great Britain than to Russia. The reason is to be found, not in the relative weakness of Russia (after defeat in war and revolution at home), but by something not taken account of in the formal agreement.

The primary aim of Izvolsky's policy was to secure the opening of the Straits at Constantinople to Russian men-of-war. As this had been consistently opposed by Great Britain throughout the nineteenth century, the Russian minister proceeded cautiously with his negotiations until he could ascertain the British views on the Straits. To his great satisfaction he learned that although certain aspects of his programme for the Straits were not acceptable, "if the negotiations now in progress between the two governments with regard to Asiatic questions had a satisfactory result, the effect upon British public opinion would be such as very much to facilitate a discussion of the Straits question if it came up later on." From that time the negotiations marched more rapidly, and Izvolsky was ready to make large concessions then in the hope of extracting other concessions later from the British about the Straits.

To this extent, then, the Anglo-Russian agreement

had more of a European point than the Anglo-French understanding. At the same time both governments assured each other and assured Germany that their accord was not directed against her. Izvolsky was indeed particular about keeping the German government informed on those points in the negotiations which affected German interests, and he declared that he was ready to negotiate a Russo-German understanding as well as an Anglo-Russian one. Yet both the British and the Russian governments had an eye on Germany in their respective policies. Even before the negotiations had begun Grey wrote: "An *entente* between Russia, France and ourselves would be absolutely secure. If it is necessary to check Germany it could then be done." And in 1908 the Russian premier, Stolypin, said that "the German frontier was his one and only thought and he was devoting all his life to make that frontier impregnable against Germany, both in men and munitions, and strategic arrangements." In short, the situation was identical with that created by the Anglo-French *entente:* Great Britain and Russia, having established cordial relations, could unite if their interests were challenged by Germany. More than that: Great Britain, France, and Russia were now closely associated, and together they could offer a formidable opposition to the Triple Alliance.

In this same year Russia and Japan, although they had recently been at war with each other, signed an agreement recognizing their respective treaty rights in China and Manchuria, while France and Japan, whose relations had been somewhat affected by the Russo-Japanese war, concluded a convention to respect the

independence and integrity of China and the principle
of the open door. Furthermore, because of events to
be described in the next chapter, Great Britain and
Spain, and France and Spain published declarations
for the maintenance of the *status quo* in the Mediterranean, and Great Britain, France and Italy concluded
an agreement for maintaining the independence and
integrity of Abyssinia. Although these four agreements lay outside the usual sphere of European politics, they had the effect of attaching Japan, Spain and
Italy in a certain measure to the Powers of the Triple
Entente. It can easily be understood that the situation thus created was not to the liking of Germany.

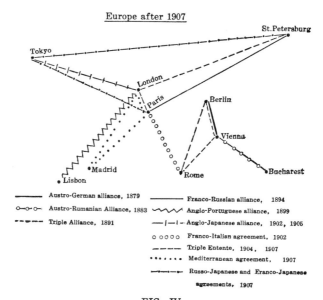

Europe after 1907

——— Austro-German alliance, 1879	——— Franco-Russian alliance, 1894
o—o—o— Austro-Rumanian Alliance, 1883	⌄⌄⌄⌄ Anglo-Portuguese alliance, 1899
━ ━ ━ ━ Triple Alliance, 1891	—|—|— Anglo-Japanese alliance, 1902, 1905

o o o o o Franco-Italian agreement, 1902
– – – – Triple Entente, 1904, 1907
• • • • • • Mediterranean agreement, 1907
—•—•—•— Russo-Japanese and Franco-Japanese
                agreements, 1907

FIG. IV

III

THE CONFLICT OF THE ALLIANCES

WHEN Lord Rosebery, who had served as British foreign secretary in 1885-86 and again in 1892-94, learned of the *Entente cordiale* in 1904, he declared to David Lloyd George, at that time an unimportant politician out of office: "It means war with Germany in the end."

GERMANY AND THE *ENTENTE;* FIRST MOROCCAN CRISIS, 1904-1905

The German government was disagreeably surprised by the Anglo-French agreement. Bülow and Holstein had convinced themselves, and they were supported by many of the German representatives abroad, that the thing was not possible. When, nevertheless, it had happened, they were rather nonplussed, and Bülow was reduced to announcing:

From the point of view of German interests we have nothing to complain of, for we do not wish to see strained relations between Great Britain and France, if only because such a state of affairs would imperil the peace of the world, the maintenance of which we sincerely desire.

The complacency thus outwardly manifested did not reflect the real sentiments of the German government, for the Emperor, the chancellor and the foreign office were much alarmed by the growing hostility of England and were disposed to ascribe the most sinister plans to King Edward VII. From the moment that the Anglo-French *entente* was announced, they began to contemplate some counter-stroke which would enable Germany to recover the advantageous position which she had previously enjoyed. But they could not agree upon the course to be pursued.

Holstein proposed to smash the new *entente* by attack on the French policy in Morocco. By the agreements of 1900 with Italy and of 1904 with Great Britain Delcassé had secured a free hand for France in Morocco, and it was obvious that France was intending to establish her control over that country, which would form the apex of her vast African Empire. Since Morocco was one of the few undeveloped countries of the world where European penetration had made little progress, Germany, whose colonial empire was very inadequate in German eyes, desired to have a hand in the game of exploiting the country; in particular the German government had its eye on the southern section, the valley of the Sus, and as the country was in a very disturbed condition an excuse for intervention would not be difficult to find. In fact German residents in Morocco had suffered much ill-treatment and no redress had been obtained. This situation seemed to offer an excellent opportunity, so Bülow and Holstein proposed to present strong demands for satisfaction to the Moroccan government and to back them up by a naval demonstration. Such action would, of course, greatly irritate the French and would open the whole Moroccan question for discussion between France and Germany. In Holstein's view, Great Britain would render only diplomatic support to France, who would then be forced to accept the German demands, for she was not strong enough to fight Germany single-handed and her ally Russia was involved in war with Japan. In consequence France would perceive that the *entente* with Great Britain was useless and would seek an understanding with Germany.

Unfortunately for Bülow and Holstein, William II refused to fall in with such plans. So far from wishing to open up a controversy with France, he was anxious to conciliate her, in order to carry through his favorite scheme for a continental alliance against Great Britain. He was willing for France to have Morocco, and had assured the King of Spain, much to the annoyance of the German foreign office, that he cherished no territorial ambitions in that country. He therefore vetoed the proposed naval demonstration.

Indeed the stars in their courses seemed to be fighting for the Emperor's plan. In October 1904 the Russian Baltic fleet, en route to Far Eastern waters, fired upon some British fishing smacks in the North Sea, and for a few days war between Great Britain and Russia appeared possible. The German government seized the opportunity to offer Russia a defensive alliance which France was to be compelled by Russia to join. The proposal was joyfully received by the Russian government—until it became evident that Great Britain was not going to fight. Then the Russians insisted that they would have to consult the French, and the Germans promptly lost interest.

William II's plan having failed, Bülow and Holstein promptly revived their own. Contending that the treaty of 1880 between the Moroccan government and various Powers, including the United States, had established the principle of equality for all Europeans in Morocco, they challenged the pretensions of the French, which by 1905 had been clearly manifested, to dictate the measures for reorganizing the Moroccan government which circumstances had made necessary. The German government denied that any rights which it possessed were affected by the Anglo-French agreement of 1904 relating to Morocco, all the more so as that agreement had never been officially communicated to it. Consequently in the winter of 1905 the relations of Germany and France became difficult. Finally in March the German Emperor was persuaded, much against his will, by Bülow to land at Tangier and make a speech in which he proclaimed that Morocco was and must remain an independent state.

The challenge to France was clear, for Delcassé's policy aimed to bring Morocco under French control. The French premier, Rouvier, was so alarmed that he began to exercise a strict control over foreign policy, and when Germany hinted and then said openly (if privately) that all would be well if Delcassé were sacrificed, Rouvier practically promised to eliminate the foreign minister. The German government thereupon demanded that France should agree to submit the

Moroccan question to an international conference, and was supported in this programme by the United States. Delcassé fought strenuously against this, for acceptance meant a double defeat: a set-back in Morocco and a humiliation at the hands of Germany, besides a weakening of the *entente;* and the British government gave him strong diplomatic support. Even Rouvier disliked the German programme, and he sought, through private emissaries, to divert the German government, offering a far-reaching programme of cooperation in other fields where French and German interests met. But Bülow and Holstein were adamant. The chief of the German general staff, Count Schlieffen, was in favor of war, Holstein was not opposed to it, and in his memoirs Bülow boasted that although he did not desire war he "did not hesitate to confront France with the question of war," trusting in his "skill and strength not to let things come to the worst." And the German government officially stated that if necessary it would stand behind Morocco "with force."

FALL OF DELCASSÉ

At the decisive meeting of the French cabinet on 6 June, Delcassé defended his policy. He declared that Germany was bluffing and that if she were not he had received from England the offer of an alliance which would permit France to accept the German challenge.[1] But his colleagues were unwilling to face

[1] The British government has denied that an alliance had been offered to France. Until the French diplomatic documents now in

the risk of war, especially as the ministers of war and marine gave discouraging reports about the fighting forces. Rouvier also voiced the view that the British were pushing France into war with Germany. The cabinet voted to accept the German programme for a conference, and Delcassé thereupon resigned. Germany had won the first round in the battle against the *Entente cordiale*. But it was a pyrrhic victory which in the end cost her dearly. It made Delcassé a martyr, for the fact that Germany had demanded his head soon became known, and it aroused the French national spirit against Germany which had for years been very little in evidence. William II's fond dreams of a Franco-German rapprochement were dealt a fatal blow, as he was soon to learn. And if at the moment the British were disgusted, the tie between England and France was in a few months reinforced. The Moroccan policy of Bülow and Holstein must be condemned as a blunder of the first magnitude.

With Delcassé removed, Rouvier expected Germany to be complacent about Morocco. Now that France had accepted the conference, he proposed that a programme be agreed upon in advance. But the German government resisted for weeks, until Theodore Roosevelt championed the French view. Even then it was not until September that a satisfactory agreement was reached. Rouvier, realizing that he had been duped, cultivated the good will of Great Britain, which was cordially manifested, and feverishly improved the mili-

course of publication are available for the year 1905, the correctness of Delcassé's statement must remain in doubt.

tary position of France. By the time the conference opened in January, 1906, France had recovered confidence and greatly strengthened her diplomatic position.

THE TREATY OF BJÖRKÖ, 1905

Meanwhile the German emperor had again tried his hand at realizing *his* plan. The defeat of Russia in the Far East and the revolutionary movement at home had reduced the Russian government to a desperate pass. Accordingly in July, 1905, William II invited Nicholas II to meet him privately in Finnish waters. Finding the Tsar much depressed, he cleverly suggested that they conclude an alliance and produced a draft treaty substantially the same as that discussed in the previous autumn. The Tsar eagerly fell in with the plan. On 24 July the treaty of Björkö providing for an alliance between Russia and Germany and the ultimate adhesion of France was signed by the two monarchs, and William II wrote a highly interesting account of the proceedings to Bülow. "My dear fatherland," he exclaimed, "is at last free from the clutch of the Franco-Russian alliance"; England's plan to isolate Germany was about to recoil on herself.[2]

The treaty might have been, as the Emperor said, "a turning point in the history of Europe," that is, if France had been willing to join it. Such a result might not have been impossible if Bülow, instead of rebuffing

[2] William II made an alteration in the draft of the treaty provided by the German foreign office which considerably altered its purpose. Bülow resigned, but consented to remain when his master melodramatically threatened suicide.

Rouvier's offer of an understanding, had exploited the French minister's suspicions of England and refrained from rattling the sabre. But by the time Lamsdorff, the Russian foreign minister, had learned of the treaty from the Tsar and had taken steps to sound the French government, the situation between France and Germany had grown so difficult that a French adhesion to the Treaty of Björkö was out of the question. As a matter of fact, Lamsdorff disliked the treaty because of his conviction that "the alliance with France is necessary to have really good relations with Germany," and he finally persuaded the Tsar that the treaty was contrary to the Franco-Russian alliance.   Nicholas thereupon notified William that the treaty would have to be amended; which the latter refused. And there the matter ended. Or rather it did not. For Russia, in order to relieve the fears of the French, prepared to give her ally unflinching support at the forthcoming conference on Morocco, and began to consider sympathetically the possibility of an understanding with Great Britain. Once again Germany had overreached herself.

ANGLO-FRENCH MILITARY CONVERSATIONS, 1906

Before the conference on Morocco opened, the Conservative government in Great Britain was replaced by a Liberal administration (December, 1905). Lansdowne, who had negotiated the *Entente cordiale,* was replaced by Sir Edward Grey. What situation might develop at the conference, no one could predict, and the French government endeavored to secure a formal promise of assistance. This Grey refused to give. He could not give it, he said, without the approval of the cabinet, and that it would amount to changing the *entente* into a defensive alliance, which would require the assent of parliament—and this, he knew, was not to be had. France would have to wait until "the pressure of circumstances—the activity of Germany, for instance—" created a situation out of which an alliance might arise—and Grey stood by this until August, 1914.[3] But if he refused to answer "the great question" to the entire satisfaction of France, he did authorize military conversations to be carried on between the British and French general staffs, so that in the event of the British government deciding to support France in war, the two armies could co-operate effectively. Grey took this step after consulting the prime minister, but the cabinet was not informed until some years later. It could be justified on the ground that the conversations were expressly declared not to be binding on the two governments, which were left free to decide their policies as circumstances required.

Nevertheless, as Winston Churchill has remarked,

Henceforth the relations of the two staffs became increasingly intimate and confidential. . . . However explicitly the two governments might agree and affirm to each other that no national or political engagement was involved in these technical discussions, the fact remained that they constituted an exceedingly potent tie.

[3] Grey's private opinion was that "if there is a war between France and Germany, it will be very difficult for us to keep out of it," but he did not admit this to the French.

The French general staff, in formulating its plans, took the chance that the British army would play a certain rôle. The British soldiers reorganized their army in order that it might participate in a European war and also began conversations with the Belgian general staff concerning the assistance which Great Britain might offer if the neutrality of Belgium were violated by Germany. The British government undoubtedly believed that it retained liberty of action, but its attitude gave the French some encouragement to hope that, if the emergency ever arose, the British army would play the part assigned to it by the two general staffs. In this fashion, a second stage in the development of the *Entente cordiale* was reached.

THE ALGECIRAS CONFERENCE

This strengthening was clearly demonstrated at the conference on Morocco which met at Algeciras from January to April, 1906. The British representative steadfastly supported the French programme and by his superior diplomatic skill placed the German delegates in a difficult position. Russia, Italy and the United States also stood by France. Germany, in short, could count only on her closest ally, Austria-Hungary, and Morocco. Holstein was in favor of imposing the German programme if need be by force, but first Bülow and then the German Emperor refused to countenance war. The French made some concessions which saved Germany's face, but secured substantially what they wanted. Delcassé's contention of the year before, that Germany would not fight for Morocco, if England and France called her bluff, was in fact substantiated. Holstein resigned in disgust, but that could not conceal the German diplomatic defeat.

Germany herself was largely to blame. Her policy was so obviously designed to destroy the *entente* between England and France that those powers necessarily drew closer together, and the veiled threat of force inevitably produced military conversations between their general staffs. Bismarck, it is true, had rattled the sabre on occasion, but his successors failed to see that the European situation in 1905-1906 was very different from that of 1875 or 1887, and they lacked the great chancellor's ingenuity for escaping from impossible situations.

William II had tried to win over the Tsar. Bülow and Holstein had tried to terrorize France. As a last resort German policy now addressed itself to Great Britain. In 1906 a number of overtures were made, but the British were cold. For a reduction in the British naval programme had been met by an increase in the German. Moreover the negotiations for an entente with Russia were under way. The German Emperor described the situation exactly: "A nice outlook! We must bargain in the future with the Franco-Russian alliance, the Anglo-French entente, and an Anglo-Russian entente, with Spain, Italy and Portugal as secondary satellites."

After 1907 the Triple *Entente* was potentially a formidable obstacle to the policy of the Triple Al-

liance. But some years had to pass before it became
a close-knit combination and then only because of im-
pulsion from without. In this development the Bosnian
crisis of 1908-1909 represented the first stage.

THE ANNEXATION OF BOSNIA, 1908

Under the Treaty of Berlin (1878) Austria-Hungary
had been empowered to "occupy and administer" the
Turkish provinces of Bosnia and Herzegovina. For
all practical purposes the provinces thereafter formed
part of the Habsburg Monarchy, but sovereignty continued to rest with the Sultan. Russia had several
times conceded that Austria might annex the territories
at an opportune moment, but in her agreement with
Austria in 1897 she had stipulated that annexation
"would require special scrutiny at the proper time and
places." By 1908 the moment had seemingly arrived.
The Austrian foreign minister, Baron Aehrenthal, was
anxious to use the opportunity offered by the Young
Turk revolution to get rid of Turkish suzerainty. The
Russian foreign minister, Izvolsky, was equally keen
to use the same opportunity to secure the opening of
the Straits for Russian men-of-war. The two statesmen met in September, 1908, at Buchlau and struck
a bargain: Austria promised not to oppose the Russian
plans at the Straits, provided Constantinople was left
to Turkey; Russia agreed to the annexation of Bosnia.
But when the Austrian government proclaimed the annexation of Bosnia on 6 October, Izvolsky asserted that
he had not understood this action to be imminent and,

not having yet secured the consent of other Powers to his Straits programme, insisted that the annexation must be referred to a European conference. Aehrenthal retorted that he had informed the Russian minister of the impending annexation and refused to allow the question to be referred to a conference unless the annexation were agreed to beforehand.[4]

This controversy between two statesmen who accused each other of lying precipitated a dangerous crisis that brought Europe to the verge of war. Izvolsky would not recognize the annexation; Aehrenthal would not agree to a free conference. The question was further complicated by the claims of Serbia for compensation. The population of Bosnia and Herzegovina was largely Serb, and Serbia had long looked forward to the day when the Austrian "occupation" should cease and the provinces should be united with Serbia. As this prospect was seemingly ruined for ever by the annexation, Serbia demanded part of the provinces as compensation. Izvolsky was compelled by Russian opinion to support this demand, all the more so since he had failed to secure from Great Britain an unqualified acceptance of his Straits programme. Aehrenthal resolutely refused to hear of compensation, for a principal motive for the annexation had been to demonstrate to Serbia her powerlessness and thus to deal a death blow to the Pan-Serb agitation in Bosnia. Thus a complete deadlock resulted between Austria and Rus-

[4] What was said by Aehrenthal and Izvolsky to each other at Buchlau remains the subject of much controversy, which can hardly be settled until the Russian documents for the time are published.

sia. In both countries certain military preparations were made, while in Austria the military party pressed for war against Serbia. By March, 1909, the tension had nearly reached the breaking-point.

The outcome of the crisis was determined by the working of the alliances. Several months before the annexation was proclaimed, Bülow, only too well aware of the isolation of Germany, had assured Aehrenthal that "the needs, interests and wishes of Austria-Hungary must be decisive for our attitude in all Balkan questions," and so sure did the Austrian minister feel of German support that he formulated his policy without consulting the German government. When the annexation was announced, the German Emperor was furious—by a combination of unlucky circumstances he heard of it only as *fait accompli*—for it meant the collapse of twenty years' effort to establish German influence in Turkey, and he was prepared to let Austria face the consequences. Bülow, however, succeeded in converting his master to his point of view, and supported Aehrenthal against Izvolsky through thick and thin. The chiefs of the Austrian and German general staffs exchanged letters, with the approval of their emperors, on the military situation, and General von Moltke (a nephew of the great Moltke) agreed that if Austria invaded Serbia and Russia intervened in consequence "this would create the *casus fœderis* for Germany," and that "at the same moment that Russia mobilizes, Germany will also mobilize and will mobilize her entire army." Bismarck had always declared that if Austria provoked Russia by her Balkan policy she could not count on German assistance. Bülow abandoned this policy and gave Vienna *carte blanche*. By the end of March Austria was in fact preparing to invade Serbia unless Serbia renounced her claims to compensation.

Izvolsky was not able to secure any such unqualified support from France and Great Britain. France, indeed, was in serious difficulties with Germany over Morocco in the autumn of 1908 (the Casablanca incident), and moreover was suspicious of Russian policy, for Izvolsky's bargaining with Aehrenthal at Buchlau had been carried on behind the back of France. The French government appears to have made clear to its ally that it did not wish to be drawn into war over the Bosnian question. Without French support, Russia obviously could not face war with Austria and Germany. Great Britain gave Russia complete diplomatic support on the question of the conference and of compensation for Serbia, for Grey deeply resented Aehrenthal's action in tearing up the Treaty of Berlin singlehanded. But more than diplomatic support the British government would not, probably could not, promise.

Thus Izvolsky was gradually pressed to the wall. As the possibility of an Austrian attack on Serbia loomed nearer, the Russian minister, realizing that Russia could not go to war (on that his military advisers were agreed), decided to abandon Serbia and in fact advised her to submit, gilding the pill by holding out hopes of assistance in the future when Russia would be strong enough to speak in a manner worthy of her.

At this moment the German government decided to

take a hand. It suggested that the Powers might recognize the annexation by an exchange of notes (instead of by a conference), provided Russia would promise beforehand to do so if she were asked by Austria. Izvolsky was inclined to accept this scheme, but gave an evasive reply, although he had reached the decision to abandon Serbia. Before this decision had become known, the German government, irritated by Izvolsky's hesitation and knowing that the military party in Vienna had got the upper hand, sent a note to the Russian government requiring an answer, "yes or no." "We must," the note continued, "regard any evasive, conditional or unclear answer as a refusal. We should then draw back and let things take their course. The responsibility for further events would then fall exclusively on M. Izvolsky."

The Russian minister was so terrified by this communication that, without consulting the French and British governments, he at once gave the necessary answer in the affirmative. He always insisted that the note had the character, though not the form, of an ultimatum, and he never forgave Germany for it, nor for that matter, Aehrenthal, whom he held responsible for all his troubles. The German government denied that its step was an ultimatum and declared that it had rendered Izvolsky a great service by preventing an Austro-Serbian war. As Kiderlen-Waechter, the author of the note, who later became German foreign minister, boasted of its strong language and was congratulated by Holstein on it, the Russian version seems nearer the truth. Certainly that version was accepted by Russian opinion, and Bülow, who also boasted of the performance, later advised William II not to repeat it. Interestingly enough, the British government refused to accept the German argument that it would be responsible for peace or war, and it declined to give assurances that it would recognize the annexation until convinced that Austria would not go to war with Serbia. If Izvolsky had not been so precipitate and had consulted his British and French colleagues, the united front of the Triple *Entente* might have caused the story to end differently. As it was, Serbia, abandoned by Russia, had to address to the Powers (not to Austria alone) a note in which she recognized that "she has not been affected in her rights by the *fait accompli* created in Bosnia" and undertook "moreover, to modify the direction of her present policy towards Austria-Hungary, and to live in future on good neighborly terms with the latter."

For the moment the Triple Alliance had asserted itself successfully against the Triple *Entente*. A year later William II declared that he had stood by his ally in "shining armor," and Bülow, writing in 1913, asserted that "by means of our strength as a continental power, we tore the web which encompassed us." Nothing was further from the facts. Izvolsky later remarked that "Russia so little got over her diplomatic defeat that she formed still closer relations with France and England." In France the opinion prevailed that "the western Powers, together with Russia, must now pay attention to their armed forces in order to be able . . . to restore the political balance which has been displaced in favor of Germany and Austria." In keeping with this, Russia in 1909 embarked on a thoroughgoing reorganization and expansion of her army, and the British government doubled its programme of naval construction in order definitely to retain the lead on Germany. Once again Germany had won a pyrrhic victory.

GERMANY'S NEW POLICY, 1909-1911

Nevertheless the situation, though uncomfortable for her, was not hopeless, and the resignation of Bülow in July, 1909, somewhat relieved the strain. His successor, Bethmann-Hollweg, was a conscientious bureaucrat who had risen to be minister of the interior. Though he had no knowledge of foreign politics, he was honest, sincerely desired to avoid war, and appreciated the consequences of the policy which Bülow had pursued for twelve years. It was necessary, he saw, for Germany to improve her relations with one or more of the *Entente* Powers, and in the course of the next three years Bethmann sedulously worked to this end.

Since Grey had declared that "there is nothing in our agreements with France and Russia which is directed against Germany and therefore nothing to bar a friendly agreement with Germany," obviously Great Britain was the power to approach first. Even Bülow, just before he fell, had come to see the desirability of an understanding on naval policy with England, for naval rivalry was the principal cause of British suspicions. Tirpitz had always opposed such an understanding, arguing that only the existence of a powerful German fleet would cause England to treat Germany with proper respect and deter her from a preventive war; with the Emperor's support, Tirpitz had resisted all suggestions for a limitation of naval armaments. Bethmann, however, insisted on opening negotiations, his position being that Germany could afford to reduce her building programme if Great Britain would promise to remain neutral in a European war. As the British were unwilling to give such a promise, nothing came of the negotiations, but they did help create a friendlier feeling between the two governments.

With Russia the German chancellor was more successful. Izvolsky was replaced in 1910 by Sazonov, and the Tsar, accompanied by his new minister, visited the German Emperor in November. At Potsdam an agreement was reached whereby Russia gave up her opposition to the Bagdad Railway, while Germany gave assurances that Austria was not pursuing an aggressive policy in Balkan questions. The two governments indeed assured each other that "neither Power is committed to any combination which might have an aggressive point directed against the other." This Potsdam agreement caused considerable commotion in both England and France where it was feared that Russia had slyly sold out her partners in the Triple *Entente*.

Towards France a good beginning was also made. In February, 1909, Bülow, after having for five years opposed the French in Morocco, suddenly reversed himself and concluded an agreement for the joint economic exploitation of Morocco by France and Germany. Consequently no objection was raised in Berlin when France proceeded to assert her political influence in Morocco. But though various schemes of joint economic activity were proposed, they all broke down, and by the spring of 1911 it looked as if France was about to establish her control over Morocco without Germany having got any material advantage. From the diplomatic point of view the German government was in a strong position to force France to bargain.

SECOND MOROCCAN CRISIS: AGADIR, 1911

But just at this moment the German government, forgetful of the lesson of 1905-1906, made a fatal blunder, or rather Kiderlen, who had been appointed foreign minister in 1910, did. Kiderlen had entered the diplomatic service in the days of Bismarck, and being a clever man, had come to fancy himself a second Bismarck. It was he who drafted the note which caused Russia to submit in March, 1909, and the momentary success apparently went to his head. When it appeared in April that the French intended, as a result of internal disturbances in Morocco, to occupy Fez, the capital, Kiderlen decided that once there, the French would not leave and that they must be brought to terms by a military demonstration. He accordingly evolved a plan for sending warships to Agadir, the port of the Sus valley which was ardently desired by many Germans; this move, he thought, would force France to make an offer of compensation which, in Kiderlen's mind, would take the form of the French Congo (though he may also have thought of the Sus valley). The Emperor, as opposed as ever to a forward Moroccan policy, reluctantly consented to the plan.

On 1 July, 1911, the gunboat *Panther* appeared at Agadir, and the Powers were notified that its presence was necessary to "lend help and assistance, in case of need, to [German] subjects and employees" there. The French case in Morocco was not a strong one, objectively considered, but since it was notorious that there were no Germans at Agadir, for the port was not open to foreigners, the German action was obviously an effort to dragoon France into submission, after the manner of 1905. In short, a new European crisis, the third since 1905, was precipitated which lasted for several months. The French were at first disposed to send warships of their own to Agadir, but then wisely decided to leave the next move to Germany. Kiderlen had not expected this and was forced to intimate that Germany expected the French Congo as the price of allowing France to have Morocco. When the French bluntly refused to hear of such compensation, Kiderlen had to face the alternative of retreat or war. He was personally ready for war, but both the chancellor and the Emperor were opposed, and as Bethmann declined to accept Kiderlen's resignation, the foreign minister perforce had to retreat. Once this vital issue was settled, Kiderlen entered on long negotiations with Jules Cambon, the French ambassador in Berlin, which, after several interruptions and near-ruptures, culminated, on 4 November, 1911, in a Franco-German agreement. By this agreement Germany recognized the French protectorate over Morocco and secured in return sections of the French Congo. German opinion was roundly dissatisfied with the small results achieved after so much bluster and four months of acute tension, and the colonial minister resigned in disgust. But instead of fixing the blame where it really belonged, on the mistaken, brutal tactics of Kiderlen, Germans generally held England responsible for the fiasco.

The British government was greatly disturbed by the appearance of the *Panther* at Agadir, for it suspected that Germany was seeking a foothold in Morocco. Grey therefore informed the German government that "a new situation had arisen" and that "we could not recognize any new arrangement which was come to without us." Bethmann and Kiderlen, intent on negotiating directly with France in the expectation of getting more from her, refused to explain that Germany expected compensation not in Morocco but in the Congo (to which England had no objection), and when the extent of the German demands in the Congo became known, with every indication that France would reject them, British suspicions of Germany became very deep. Prompt action was accordingly taken. The military conversations between the British and French general staffs, which had been proceeding leisurely for some years, were brought to a head (20 July), and the details settled of the plan for the British army to fight by the side of the French.

Precautions were also taken in the British navy. This, of course, was not known at the time, but nothing could have caused greater excitement than the speech delivered by Mr. Lloyd George, the chancellor of the exchequer, on the evening of 21 July. He was known as an advocate of friendly relations with Germany and as an opponent of naval expenditure. When therefore he said that Britain could not be ignored "when her interests were vitally affected, as if she were of no account in the cabinet of nations" and that "peace at that price would be a humiliation intolerable for a great country like ours to endure," his meaning was only too clear—and Germany understood it. While the air was tense for a few days, satisfactory explanations of German policy were soon forthcoming, and the danger of war disappeared. Later when the French proposed to send warships to Morocco if the Germans landed at Agadir, the British government exercised a restraining influence.

At the moment the Lloyd George speech was as successful in clearing the air as was the German action at St. Petersburg in March, 1909, but in the long run its effects were as disastrous as William II's speech at Tangier. Because Germans generally ascribed their diplomatic defeat to British intervention, Tirpitz drew the conclusion that the German navy should be increased. In spite of Bethmann's opposition, the Emperor approved Tirpitz's plans, and early in 1912 it became known that a new German navy bill would be introduced, although assurances had previously been given to the British government that the programme laid down in 1900, 1906 and 1908 would not be exceeded.

THE HALDANE MISSION, 1912

Before the bill was published, a last effort was made by the two governments to reach an understanding. At German suggestion, inspired perhaps by Bethmann, Lord Haldane, the British minister of war, who was known for his German sympathies and was supposed to understand the Germans well, journeyed to Berlin to explore the possibilities of agreement. In the course of conversations with William II, Tirpitz and Bethmann he was given to understand that Germany would be willing to retard her contemplated additional building programme if Great Britain would give an undertaking to remain neutral if war were forced upon Germany. The British government found the German offer unsatisfactory. The admiralty thought the naval concessions inadequate, the foreign office was unwilling to promise unconditional neutrality because that would involve sacrificing the *entente* with France— which was, in fact, the German aim. Grey finally proposed the following formula:

The two Powers being mutually desirous of securing peace and friendship between them, England declares that she will neither make nor join in any unprovoked attack upon Germany and pursue no aggressive policy towards her.

Aggression upon Germany is not the subject and forms no part of any treaty, understanding, or combination to which England is now a party, nor will she become a party to anything that has such an object.

Bethmann declared the formula unsatisfactory unless a clause were added providing for British neutrality if war were forced upon Germany. The negotiations then came to an end, to the great relief of the French, whose suspicions were shared by the officials of the British foreign office.

This episode, in which the motive of both powers appear to have been sincere, illustrates the vicious circle in which all were caught by the system of alliances and the burden of armaments. The British wished to limit armaments, which were both dangerous and expensive. The Germans said: Situated as we are between France and Russia, we cannot discuss a limitation unless Great Britain will abandon the Triple *Entente*. To this the British replied: We cannot abandon the *Entente* if you continue to add to your navy, for you have the Triple Alliance. Tirpitz might have yielded on the fleet in return for a promise of unconditional neutrality. Such a promise Grey could not give, partly because of British obligations to Belgium (and German plans to invade Belgium were deeply suspected), partly because British interests would not permit giving Germany a free hand to deal with France. Great Britain insisted on her naval superiority and her diplomatic combinations, which maintained the balance in her favor. To restore the balance, Germany had to retain freedom in armaments or break up the *Entente*. The problem was as Bethmann said, "insoluble."

Germany's difficulty was, in fact, two-fold. The rapid increase of her population (from 40,000,000 in 1871 to 65,000,000 in 1910), the phenomenal development of industry and expansion of her foreign trade, the might of her army and the building of her fleet upset the European equilibrium as it had existed from 1815 to 1870. The creation of a counter-balance was unavoidable and necessary—at least in the eyes of other states. And precisely because Germany, in her logical efforts to secure for herself a "place in the sun," had come up against the interests of Great Britain, France and Russia in Africa and the Near East, interests which usually antedated the claims of Germany, those powers instinctively drew together, and their instincts were strengthened by the provocative methods of German diplomacy and the flamboyant speeches of the German Emperor.

Of all this Bethmann was only too painfully aware, and hence his efforts to "break the ring." But it was the pacific chancellor's misfortunes that he was not strong enough to control the political situation in his country. He could not impose a clear-cut programme on the German people because they themselves were not united. To the soldiers, France was the Power to be reckoned with, to the sailors Great Britain. Big business and high finance preferred expansion in the Near East, which was calculated to provoke Russia. A wise government would have made a choice between the several possible courses, but the German government actually pursued all three courses at once. Neither the Emperor, the chancellor nor Tirpitz could entirely prevail. Jules Cambon, the experienced French ambassador, was entirely right in saying that however well organized the German political and economic machine might be as a whole, there was "anarchy" in the highest circles. Consequently Bethmann, though he negotiated with Great Britain, Russia and France in turn, was never able to offer any one of them sufficient inducement to relax its association with the other two; while the very fact that he endeavored to wean away first one and then another in the end only deepened the suspicions which all three felt concerning the ultimate aim of German policy.

CONSOLIDATION OF THE TRIPLE *ENTENTE*, 1912-1914

So it came about that from 1912 to 1914 the Triple *Entente* was steadily tightened. If France had been lukewarm in her support of Russia during the Bosnian crisis, Russia had at the time of Agadir urged France to compromise with Germany. But as the Italian attack on Tripoli in September, 1911, threatened to open up the Near Eastern question, it was high time for the two allies to concert their policies together, and in February, 1912, the Russian government proposed a discussion with France. By this time Raymond Poincaré had become French premier and minister of foreign affairs (January, 1912). Poincaré was an eminent lawyer who wished precision in all things. On the one hand, he feared that Germany might some day repeat the tactics of Agadir, and he realized that with the Moroccan question settled France's position in European politics depended on the solidity of her alliance with Russia; without this France could not stand up against Germany. On the other hand this meant, in practice, that France must be prepared to support Russian policy in the Near East, which might involve France in a European war. Poincaré therefore faced the double task of exercising some control over Russian policy and of persuading French opinion of the necessity of supporting Russia to the limit. The latter task was accomplished partly by the personality of Poincaré himself, whose honesty gave him a strong hold on the French public, partly by the bribery of certain newspapers, for which the money was furnished by the Russian government. By September, 1912, Izvolsky, now ambassador in Paris, was able to report that if Russia became involved in war with Austria as the result of Austria's attacking Serbia, and this in turn led to German intervention, France would recognize the *casus fœderis*.

France [said Poincaré] is incontestably disposed to peace and neither seeks nor desires war, but the intervention of Germany against Russia would immediately modify this state of mind . . . in such case parliament and public opinion would entirely approve the decision of the government to lend armed support to Russia.

The year 1912 was indeed marked by a considerable revival of French patriotic and national feeling, for which Agadir was in no small measure responsible.

In his second task Poincaré was less successful. Though he visited Russia in August, 1912, and had long conversations with Sazonov which resulted in a general agreement on policies, the French minister was disconcerted by the exact terms, which he learned for the first time, of the secret treaty between Serbia and

Bulgaria (March, 1912), which had been negotiated under Russian auspices and which portended a Balkan attack on Turkey. Poincaré made heroic, but unsuccessful, efforts to prevent the outbreak of the Balkan war in October. Thereafter he repeatedly insisted, as did his successors, that Russia must consult France in advance about her policy. France was willing to fulfil the obligations of her alliance, but only within the terms of the treaty and provided she had consented to the Russian action. More than once during 1912-1913 the French government successfully restrained Russia from isolated or premature action, and it exerted pressure on Serbia to prevent that little state from pushing home its quarrel with Austria and thus precipitating Russian action against Austria. Nevertheless it is clear that the Franco-Russian alliance had ceased to be a strictly passive instrument. France did not indeed go so far with respect to Russia as did Germany in 1909 when she gave Austria a free hand against Serbia, but the spirit of the military convention of 1892 was altered. France could still advise her ally against any action which might lead to war, but she had promised, in case she agreed to the proposed policy, to accept the consequences.

In keeping with the new situation, the French and Russian general staffs, in annual conferences, revised their plans for common action in the event of war. They agreed that both armies should assume the offensive and that Russia should hasten the construction of strategic railways in Poland, the money for which would be provided by French loans. In the summer of

1912 a naval convention was negotiated between the two governments. Finally in 1913 France restored three years as the term of military service, and Russia added to the strength of her army. Just as the diplomacy of Poincaré revived the international prestige of France, so the military reforms created in professional circles a feeling of confidence which had hitherto been lacking. Although occasional disagreements occurred, in general France and Russia in 1913-1914 functioned as a unit in all the wearisome disputes of the Balkan wars and their aftermath. Since their point of view was usually in sharp opposition to that of the Triple Alliance, the division of Europe into two rival camps was accentuated and the danger of a universal conflict increased.

Great Britain was also forced by circumstances into a closer connection with her associates of the *Entente*. When the Haldane mission brought no fruits and the German government proceeded with its new naval bill, the British admiralty deemed it necessary, in order to meet the German challenge in the North Sea, to withdraw certain ships from the Mediterranean, where in consequence the combined fleets of Austria and Italy would obtain the ascendency. The problem could be solved by concentrating the French fleet, which had been divided with Brest and Toulon, in the Mediterranean. The French were quite willing to do this, but they saw an opportunity to secure from the British a more definite promise of assistance than they had hitherto been able to obtain. If, they said to the British, we withdraw our ships from the Channel, we must have some assurance that our northern coasts will be protected in the event of war with Germany. The British government admitted the force of the argument and consented to an exchange of notes, which took place in November, 1912. The essential portion of the notes read:

If either government had grave reason to expect an unprovoked attack by a third power, or something that threatened the general peace, it should immediately discuss with the other whether both governments should act together to prevent aggression and to preserve peace, and if so, what measures they would be prepared to take in common. If those measures involved action, the plans of the general staff would at once be taken into consideration, and the governments would then decide what effect should be given to them.

In the eyes of the British cabinet, this was intended to put on record the fact that the British government was still free to act as it thought best in the time of crisis (so Grey states in his memoirs), but Poincaré informed his colleagues that the notes "established the principle of an eventual cooperation of the military and naval forces of France and England." Plans for naval cooperation, comparable to those for the two armies, were in fact devised and extended to Far Eastern waters.[5]

That the British still considered themselves unbound was to be attested by their hesitations in July, 1914. But they did impose upon themselves a moral obliga-

[5] The French general staff wished to consider the possibility of sending troops into Belgium in the event that German troops concentrated in large numbers along the eastern frontier of Belgium. But the British objected, and the idea was dropped.

tion. They were, in fact, caught in a difficult situation.
Because they genuinely feared aggressive action on the
part of Germany, it was elementary common sense to
take precautions which would enable them and the
French to meet the situation effectively. Yet an open
and formal alliance would have been rejected by parliament and the country. In consequence the cabinet
fell back on a policy which, as Winston Churchill said,
had "the obligations of an alliance without its advan-
tages and above all without its precise definitions."
The government could assure the country that its hands
were free—and thus encourage Germany to gamble on
British neutrality. Yet the French were equally encouraged to gamble on British participation in a war
which might result.

British relations with Russia never reached the same
degree of intimacy as those with France. This was
partly because British public opinion did not regard
questions of the Near East, which were of vital concern to Russia, as falling within the scope of British
interests which might be worth fighting for, partly because Russian activity in Persia caused considerable
concern to Great Britain and often seemed not in harmony with the Anglo-Russian convention of 1907.
During the Balkan crisis of 1912-13, British diplomacy
exerted itself to mediate between Russian and Austrian
claims, and Grey refused to commit himself on the
question whether Great Britain would take part in a
European war arising out of the Balkans. Likewise
in the winter of 1913-14, when the Russian government
became greatly excited over the sending of a German

military mission to Turkey, Grey did not give whole-hearted support to the Russian protest.

In the spring of 1914, however, a new turn was given to Anglo-Russian relations when Sazonov suggested that the Triple *Entente* should be converted into a formal alliance, which should be published. Grey was of the opinion that the political situation in England would not permit such a step, but, at the wish of the French, he agreed to communicate to the Russian government the notes which had been exchanged between Great Britain and France in November, 1912. He also consented that conversations should be begun between the British and Russian admiralties, analogous to those between the British and French military and naval experts. The situation was accurately described by Grey when, in June, 1914, he said to the German ambassador in London that "though we were not bound by engagement [to France and Russia] as allies, we did from time to time talk as intimately as allies." Indeed, early in July, 1914, when Sazonov once more adverted to the idea of an alliance, Grey replied that he was "personally attracted" by it and would consult his colleagues as soon as the Irish situation permitted. The general attitude of the British foreign office was reflected by a departmental minute of 20 July: "Russia is a formidable power and will become unceasingly strong. Let us hope that our relations with her will continue to be friendly."

If the powers of the Triple *Entente* were more closely united in July, 1914, than at any previous time, the same was seemingly true of the Triple Alliance. In the Balkan crisis of 1912-13 Germany had resolutely supported Austria-Hungary in forbidding Serbia to secure an outlet on the Adriatic.   True, Germany had later counselled moderation and had vetoed the Austrian wish, in July, 1913, to save Bulgaria by an action against Serbia.   But in October, 1913, William II had promised Conrad, the Austrian chief of staff, that if Austria marched against Serbia, "I'll go with you"; and to Berchtold, the Austrian foreign minister, he said, "I stand behind you, and am ready to draw the sabre if ever your action makes it necessary."   The Austrians were justified in thinking that they had only to seize the first opportunity offered for a reckoning with Serbia.

The Balkan wars had also had the effect of bringing Italy back into the fold.   The Triple Alliance was formally renewed in December, 1912, a year and a half before its expiration, and Italy had stood with Austria in opposing the Serbian claims on the Adriatic.   Although Italy and Austria continued to be suspicious of each other in Albania, a naval convention was negotiated between the three powers of the alliance which provided that

the naval forces of the Triple Alliance which may be in the Mediterranean shall unite for the purpose of gaining naval control of the Mediterranean by defeating the enemy fleets.

This convention went into effect on 1 November, 1913, and was declared "valid for 1914." In addition, an agreement was reached in March, 1914, between Germany and Italy, by which Italy pledged herself to send three army corps and two cavalry divisions to the German army in the event of war with France. Moltke endeavored to convince his skeptical Austrian colleague that Italy could be relied upon to keep her engagements, and himself later wrote: "All these agreements were made so clear and so binding that a doubt of Italy's loyalty to the alliance could hardly arise." Whether the German and Austrian foreign offices were equally optimistic may be open to doubt, but the fact remains that in 1914 the military and naval arrangements of the Triple Alliance were more complete and extensive than at any time in its history. Its actual military power was also greater than ever, for Germany had, in 1913, greatly increased the strength of her standing army and made enormous additions to its material equipment, levying a special tax for the purpose. In smaller degree her example had been followed by her two allies. And the German general staff, at any rate, was confident of victory in the event of war.

THE SCHISM OF EUROPE

Thus in 1914 the two rival diplomatic groups stood face to face. Was war the inevitable or necessary consequence of this schism of Europe? At the moment there was no immediate prospect of it. In spite of the failure of the Haldane mission and of the German navy law of 1912, the British and German governments had reached an informal understanding concerning the construction of battleships in the ratio of 16:10. They had co-operated during the Balkan wars in restraining Russia and Austria respectively. Most important of all, they had negotiated two agreements liquidating their differences in Africa and with respect to the Bagdad Railway. The agreements had not been formally signed, but they had created a feeling in Germany that England would not "in all circumstances take the side of France," but because of the German fleet "will consider very seriously whether it is then so safe and simple to play the part of France's guardian angel against us."

Between Germany and France there were no difficulties pending, for in February, 1914, they had come to terms about their spheres of economic influence and railway schemes in Turkey. A little later Poincaré, now president of the Republic, had dined at the German Embassy, thereby breaking a tradition of more than forty years. Alsace-Lorraine had assuredly not been forgotten. But the German ambassador wrote in February, 1914:

The desire for military revenge, as it was incorporated in Boulanger and Déroulède, is a stage that is passed. It exists to-day, to be sure, but only in a theatrical sense. The wound of 1871 still burns in all French hearts, but no one is disposed to risk his or his sons' necks for the question of Alsace-Lorraine; a constellation would have to be set up which offered quite favorable and even easy prospects for the success of such a gamble. But this is becoming ever more unlikely. The hopes of reaching the goal through the help of Russia have long since proved deceptive. . . . The idea is spreading more and more that the salvation of France must be sought in a better relationship with Germany.

The elections of May, 1914, were strongly in favor of the Left parties, who wished to abolish the three years' military service restored in the previous year. When they formed a government they were with difficulty persuaded to let the law stand till an adequate new system could be devised. It cannot be said that in either Great Britain or France in 1914 was war with Germany arising out of a direct quarrel regarded as inevitable.

The real danger to the peace of Europe was in the Near East. Russia's primary interest lay at the Straits, and the Russian government had considered the matter very thoroughly in the winter of 1913-14. In Sazonov's opinion the best policy for Russia was to preserve the *status quo* as long as possible, i.e., to maintain Turkey in the condition in which she emerged from the Balkan wars, "neither too strong nor too weak," strong enough to keep alive, weak enough to have, in the end, to accept Russia's proposals for opening the Straits. On these terms, Turkey might retain Constantinople. But Russia could not allow any other power to possess the Straits. Therefore plans were discussed for seizing the Straits by a *coup de main* if necessary. As the military and naval authorities were agreed that Russia was not then in a position to execute such a stroke and could do so in any case only in the complications offered by a general war, they were ordered to prepare plans. But practically nothing had been done by the summer of 1914.

What worried the Russians was the steady advance of German influence in Turkey. Between the military mission sent out late in 1913 to reorganize the Turkish army and the Bagdad Railway, Germany bade fair to become the political and economic master of the Ottoman Empire, to establish a control not unlike the British occupation of Egypt. With the assistance of Germany, Turkey would become so strong that she could resist Russian demands for the opening of the Straits. Thus German and Russian interests were diametrically opposed, and some day they might clash openly.

In the Balkan peninsula the protagonists were Russia and Austria-Hungary. The former was promoting the closest relations between Rumania, Serbia and Greece, who had despoiled Bulgaria in the second Balkan war and were determined to maintain the Treaty of Bucharest. The existence of such a combination would greatly lighten Russia's task when she raised the question of the Straits and also serve as a barrier to the supposed ambitions of Austria. Austria, for her part, was anxious to create a Balkan league of her own of Rumania, Greece, and Bulgaria which would isolate Serbia; Bulgaria was asking to be taken into the Triple Alliance, but Germany was hesitant, because King Ferdinand was not trusted. Turkey was also friendly to the Triple Alliance, and had agreed, in principle, to an alliance with Bulgaria.

A glance at the map will illustrate the situation clearly. Germany, Austria-Hungary, Bulgaria and

Turkey in one group: if Serbia could be brought under control, the influence of the Central Powers would extend from Berlin to the Persian Gulf, and Russia would be helpless behind the Straits. Russia, Rumania, Serbia, Montenegro and Greece in another group: a wedge would be driven from the Black Sea to the Adriatic between the Central Powers and their protégés, and the question of the Straits would be less difficult of solution for Russia. Thus in July, 1914, Serbia occupied the key position in European politics. Her subjection was as desirable for Germany and Austria as it was intolerable for Russia. Were the issue joined, neither side could admit defeat without seeing the balance of European power pass definitely to the other.

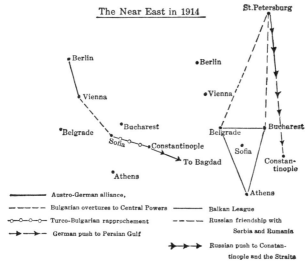

FIG. V

The only hope of forestalling a crisis was to make use of the concert of Europe. Thanks to Grey, the concert had been brought into being during the Balkan wars and had succeeded in keeping the peace between Russia and Austria. But the concert did not function automatically. It had to be created for each special case, that is, the Powers had to agree to work together, and the refusal of any one was fatal. On the eve of Sarajevo there was, however, reason to hope that in the event of a new crisis, the concert might be reconstituted. Less than two weeks before the murder the German chancellor wrote to his ambassador in London:

I do not believe that Russia is planning an early war against us. But, covered as she is by her extensive military preparations, she would certainly like, in the event of a new Balkan crisis—and we shall not be able to take it amiss—to make a stronger stand than she did in the recent Balkan complications. Whether in such a case it would come to a general European conflagration would depend exclusively on the attitude of Germany and England.

In other words, these two powers could, by means of co-operation in the concert of Europe, keep the peace, in spite of the Triple Alliance and the Triple *Entente*.

THE CRISIS OF JULY, 1914

On 28 June, 1914, the Archduke Francis Ferdinand and his wife were assassinated at Sarajevo by Gavrilo Printsip, a Serb by race but an Austro-Hungarian subject. The crisis caused by this crime, which culminated in the World War, was essentially a trial of strength between the two rival groups of Powers.

The governing classes in Austria-Hungary, chiefly Germans and Magyars, had for some years been disturbed by the restlessness of the Southern Slav peoples, which was undoubtedly stimulated by Serbia. They feared, if not the disintegration of the state, at any rate the collapse of the privileged political system of which they were the beneficiaries. They decided to seize the opportunity for the long-desired reckoning with Serbia. Believing that sooner or later war with Russia was bound to come, they preferred to have war then—for they did not expect Russia to remain indifferent—rather than later, when Russia would have completed her military reorganization. If German support could be secured, they would go to war with Serbia, crush the little country, and then, in some form or other, by a military convention or a customs union, connect it with the Austro-Hungarian monarchy. Thus they would solve the Southern Slav question, rehabilitate their prestige among the other non-German and non-Magyar races, and secure for the Dual Monarchy a firm position among the European powers.

The appeal for German support was successful. Thereupon the Austro-Hungarian government drew up a forty-eight-hour ultimatum which was intended to be rejected; proclaimed the Serbian reply, which in very large measure accepted the Austrian demands, unsatisfactory; declared war on Serbia; and rejected all proposals for compromise or the cessation of hostilities.

Russia promptly came to the assistance of Serbia, partly because the Serbs were her Slavic kinsmen, partly because she had promised Serbia in previous crises that when she was ready she "would do everything for Serbia." Sazonov vainly tried, both by direct demand on Austria and through appeals to Germany, to secure some modification of the Austrian ultimatum. To the Austrian declaration of war, Russia replied by the mobilization of her army, for the Austrian assurances that no Serbian territory would be taken were regarded as inadequate and insincere. Unless Russia were to recognize the destruction of Serbia by Austria, no other course was open to her. But in ordering mobilization, the Tsar was well aware that a European war would result, for Germany had given official notice to this effect, and his assurances that the Russian troops would not cross the frontier so long as negotiations continued, while probably sincere, were as unacceptable to Germany as were the Austrian assurances to Russia about the integrity of Serbia.

The policy of Germany was guided by two considerations. In the first place, the German government was seriously alarmed by the internal condition of Austria, which it regarded as its one reliable ally. Unless the Habsburg monarchy could be revivified Germany would find herself isolated between France and Russia. When therefore the Austrian government signified its desire to "march into Serbia," the German government at once approved and urged immediate action. Expecting Great Britain to remain neutral, it was willing to run the risk of war with Russia, because the German general staff believed that Germany and Austria could defeat Russia and France. The German government did not deliberately plan a European war—but it did put the system of alliances to the test. If Russia and France backed down without fighting, the ascendancy of the Triple Alliance would be assured for an indefinite time. Hence after the Austrian ultimatum had precipitated the crisis, Germany at first refused to hear of any proposals of mediation and incited Austria to declare war immediately, so as to stave off such proposals. But when it began to seem likely that, contrary to German calculations, Great Britain would be drawn into the war, Germany advised Austria to accept a British proposal that she should negotiate with the Powers after occupying Belgrade. Unfortunately, the German pressure was relaxed at the critical moment, probably because the military party in Berlin was insisting on war, and Austria declined the British suggestion.

At this moment the news of the Russian mobilization was received in Berlin, and the second motive of German policy began to function. Because Germany would have to fight both Russia and France, the German general staff had evolved a plan for a headlong attack on France which was expected to overwhelm the French in six weeks. That accomplished, the German armies would then be transferred to the eastern front to deal with the slowly-mobilized Russians. In German eyes, speed was the essential element in the plan, which could not succeed if Russia were given time to mobilize at leisure. The German general staff therefore insisted on making the Russian mobilization a *casus belli,* for France would at once come to the help of Russia and this would provide the excuse necessary for the German invasion of France. As was to be expected, Russia refused the German demand for instant demobilization, whereupon Germany declared war. But France, in order to avoid the appearance of an aggressor, refused to play the German game. Actually the German troops at once invaded France, and finally the German government declared war on France: which was of incalculable value to France in consolidating sentiment at home and in winning help and sympathy abroad.

The position of France was comparatively simple. Convinced that if Russia were not supported on an issue considered vital by her, she would abandon France and that France would thus be left at the mercy of a triumphant Germany, the French government stood by its ally from the beginning of the crisis. Though advising caution in the matter of military preparations, it gave every assurance that it would abide by the terms of the Franco-Russian alliance; and this assurance enabled the Russian government to take the firm stand it did. In spite of the pacific temper of the French people, public opinion supported the government, for it realized that the future of France was at stake. At the end the government did not have even to publish the terms of the alliance with Russia, which in fact remained unknown until 1918.

The crisis found the British government faced by the prospect of civil war in Ireland, a fact which may have contributed to German confidence in British neutrality. In face of the European danger, however, the Irish controversy was adjourned, and played no part in ensuing events. Grey worked sincerely for peace, making various proposals for delay, discussion and compromise, all of which were rejected by Germany and Austria. Particularly regrettable was the German refusal of a conference of ambassadors in London, the object of which was intended to delay and if possible prevent actual military operations, for once fighting started, "the dice were set rolling," as Bethmann said, and nothing could stop them. But while he was anxious to keep peace, Grey, after the Austrian ultimatum and the Serbian reply, believed that Russia could not be expected to stand aside, and he refused to compromise Great Britain in the eyes of Russia by unwelcome pressure, as Germany desired.

From the beginning of the crisis Grey was besought by Sazonov to declare British solidarity with Russia and France, on the ground that this alone would force the Central Powers to yield, that otherwise war was unavoidable, and Great Britain would have to take part. This plea was of course supported by France. It is possible that a clear-cut British declaration, if made before Austria declared war on Serbia, would have had the effect desired. But Grey could not give any promise. Although he, the prime minister and several other members of the cabinet believed that Great Britain must, in her own interests, regardless of absence of a written obligation, stand by France, the majority of the cabinet were opposed to such a course. Asquith and Grey were unwilling to take the risk of a step which might be repudiated by the house of commons. It was not until Germany had declared war on Russia and presented an ultimatum to France that a promise was given to France to defend her northern coasts if they were attacked by Germany. Even then, the promise was made dependent on the approval of parliament and could be given only because the Conservative opposition had promised to support it. Thus, at the supreme moment, the liberty of action which the British government had insisted on reserving paralyzed its action. Since Germany promised not to attack the northern coasts of France, the British promise might never have had to be made effective but for the German invasion of Belgium.

It was this which united a divided cabinet and a wavering public opinion in favor of immediate war. Grey has sometimes been reproached for not making clear to Germany much earlier than he did that Great Britain would make the violation of Belgium a *casus belli*. Probably this would have been useless. The German general staff had, at the moment, no other plan than to go through Belgium; moreover Moltke was convinced that Great Britain would enter the war regardless of Belgium, and he was not greatly worried by the prospect of British intervention because he expected to defeat the French armies decisively before the British appeared on the scene. Grey has also been criticized because he refused to formulate for Germany the conditions on which Great Britain would remain neutral. From the point of view of diplomatic technique he could not do so, for it would remove any necessity for the Central Powers to compromise. From the point of view of British interests he could not do so because, rightly or wrongly, Grey believed that German victory would establish a German hegemony in Europe which would be intolerable for Great Britain. In Grey's eyes the danger of war arose solely from the refusal of the Central Powers to negotiate. If war had to be, then Great Britain must take part in it. In such circumstances he could not stultify himself by indicating the conditions of an unthinkable neutrality. How far he was influenced by the feeling of a moral obligation to France is uncertain, but it was probably of less importance than is often asserted.

Italy, the remaining Great Power to be considered, disapproved of the Austrian action on principle and expediency alike. Remembering her own history, she did not think it possible for Austria to suppress the Southern Slav national movement by force. But in case Austria did succeed in bringing Serbia under her control, Italian interests in the Balkans would be gravely affected. Finally, Italy did not dare, because of her long coastline, expose herself to the British fleet. The Italian government therefore took advantage of the fact that, in violation of Article VII of the Triple Alliance, it had not been consulted beforehand about the Austrian action, to declare that the Central Powers were waging a war of aggression, and to proclaim her neutrality. It is not without interest to note that in spite of the formal treaty the Central Powers could not persuade Italy to march with them, whereas, in spite of the absence of any formal treaty, Great Britain did march with France and Russia. In other words, treaties concluded in one set of circumstances avail little when the circumstances have changed.

For forty-three years the peace of Europe was maintained between the Great Powers through the combined effect of alliances and armaments. In the crises prior to 1914 governments drew back at the edge of the abyss either because they were not assured of sufficient support from other governments, were not ready from a military point of view, or did not consider the issue worth fighting for. In 1914 the issue was nothing less than the balance of power in Europe for an incalculable time, and all the governments believed themselves ready. The Triple *Entente* was prepared to accept a diplomatic humiliation of Serbia, but not her military subjugation. The Triple Alliance, or rather the Central Powers, insisted on a military solution. Thus the system of alliances, designed originally as a guarantee of peace, proved, when put to the test, to be the mechanism for unchaining a general war.

Likewise great armaments proved their futility. At no time did the vast armies and navies create a feeling of security. No general staff ever admitted that its country was safe; always it clamored for more soldiers and more arms. In the end, after every increase in one country had been imitated by all other powers, the prevailing feeling was one of insecurity, as is only too well revealed by the memoirs of various generals and admirals. But few if any statesmen imagined what would be the effect of these military machines on diplomatic negotiations in the hour of crisis. So long as diplomatists merely rattled the sabre, no harm was done save to render the diplomatic situation more acute. But when governments actually began mobilizing their armies, the military timetable at once took precedence over diplomatic etiquette. No general staff could afford to let a rival get a start, and the diplomatists were shoved aside. If in July, 1914, not a man had been called up, the foreign offices would doubtless have worked out a compromise. But once mobilization began, it had automatically to run its course, and a miracle would have had to happen, once the armies were assembled facing each other, if peace were to be preserved. Armaments then, so far from ensuring peace, as their protagonists always promised, effectively prevented peace.

APPENDIX

THE GROWTH OF ARMAMENTS

ARMIES

THE German constitution of 1871 imposed the obligation of military service on every able-bodied man and fixed the strength of the standing army at one per-cent of the population. In the next few years the other Continental powers adopted the principle of conscription, only Great Britain continuing to raise her army by volunteer enlistments. The terms of service varied from three years in Germany and Austria-Hungary to five in France and six in Russia.

1875

Country	Population	Army	Percentage of Army to Population	Cost [1]
Germany	41,000,000	430,000	1.05	$96,000,000
France	36,000,000	430,000	1.25	98,750,000
Austria-Hungary	36,000,000	278,000	.8	39,000,000
Italy	27,000,000	212,000	.9	36,000,000
Russia in Europe	79,000,000	822,000	1.04	90,000,000
Russian Empire	86,000,000	846,000	.98	
Great Britain...	32,000,000	130,000	.4	73,500,000

[1] The tables are based on the *Statesman's Year Book,* and in order to facilitate comparisons, have been simplified as much as possible; all figures are given in round numbers, and currencies have been converted into dollars at the pre-war rates of exchange. "Cost" is the budget estimate. As the budgets of different countries do not always include the same items, it is difficult to calculate exactly the expenditure per head of population. The British volunteer army was paid at a much higher rate than Continental soldiers, hence the high cost in proportion to size.

1895

Country	Population	Army	Percentage of Army to Population	Cost
Germany	49,000,000	585,000 [2]	1.2	$120,000,000
France	38,000,000	572,000 [3]	1.5	130,000,000
including Algeria and Tunis	44,000,000		1.3	
Austria-Hungary	41,000,000	354,000	.84	53,000,000
Italy	30,000,000	253,000	.84	45,000,000
Russia in Europe	103,000,000	792,000	.77	90,000,000
Russian Empire	122,000,000	869,000	.71	
Great Britain...	38,000,000	155,000	.4	90,000,000

1905

Country	Population	Army	Percentage	Cost
Germany	56,000,000	614,000	1.1	187,000,000
France	39,000,000	533,000 [4]	1.37	147,000,000
including Algeria and Tunis	45,500,000	607,000	1.33	
Austria-Hungary	50,000,000	387,000	.77	60,000,000
Italy	32,500,000	265,000 [5]	.8	56,500,000
Russia in Europe	107,000,000	1,100,000 [6]	1.03	187,500,000
Russian Empire	129,000,000	1,200,000	.93	
Great Britain...	42,000,000	204,000	.49	149,000,000

1912

Country	Population	Army	Percentage	Cost
Germany	65,000,000	656,000	1.01	173,000,000
France	39,500,000	539,000	1.38	167,000,000
including Algeria and Tunis	47,000,000	613,000	1.3	
Austria-Hungary	51,000,000	396,000 [7]	.78	125,000,000
Italy	35,000,000	302,000	.87	79,000,000
Russia in Europe	136,000,000	1,225,000	.9	281,000,000
Russian Empire	164,000,000		.75	
Great Britain...	45,000,000	187,000	.4	139,000,000

[2] Term of service reduced in 1893 to two years for unmounted troops.

[3] Term of service reduced in 1889 to three years.

[4] Term of service reduced in 1905 to two years; all exemptions eliminated.

[5] Term of service reduced in 1908 to two years.

[6] Term of service reduced in 1906 to three years.

[7] Term of service reduced in 1912 to two years.

1914

Country	Population	Army	Percentage of Army to Population	Cost
Germany	65,000,000 *actual:* 761,000		1.17	$218,000,000
	planned: 830,000		1.3	
	British and French estimates: 870,000			
France	39,500,000	739,000 [8]	1.87	241,000,000
including Algeria and Tunis	47,000,000	821,000	1.77	
	German estimate: 884,000			
Austria-Hungary	51,000,000	479,000	.94	156,000,000
Italy	35,000,000	305,000	.87	94,000,000
Russia in Europe	136,000,000	1,300,000 [9]	.96	399,000,000
	German estimate: 1,539,000			
Russian Empire	164,000,000	1,445,000	.8	
Great Britain...	45,000,000	187,000	.4	139,000,000
including colonial garrisons.		248,000		

NAVIES

1880

Country	Ironclads	Total Fleet	Personnel	Cost
Great Britain......	68	248	53,600	$52,000,000
France	59	498		43,000,000
Russia	30	223		13,000,000
Germany	20	85	7,500	5,000,000
Austria-Hungary ..	14	61	6,100	4,500,000
Italy	18	88	14,200	8,500,000
United States	24	83	9,000	13,500,000
Japan	1	13	1,600	3,250,000

1890

Country	Armored	Total Fleet	Personnel	Cost
Great Britain	91	373	69,000	70,000,000
France	57	432		40,000,000
Russia	44		29,000	24,000,000
Germany	29	209	17,800	8,400,000
Austria-Hungary ..	11	117	8,500	2,300,000
Italy	21	269	21,000	22,000,000
United States	23	77	9,000	26,000,000
Japan	17	60	9,500	3,000,000

[8] Term of service raised in 1913 to three years.
[9] Term of service raised in 1913 to three and one-half years.

1900

Country	Battleships	Coast Defence	Cruisers	Destroyers	Personnel	Cost
Great Britain....	67	10	118	197	115,000	$133,000,000
France	28	18	59	192		61,000,000
Russia	28	13	23	201	40,000	44,000,000
Germany	24	19	17	146	26,500	40,000,000
Austria-Hungary	10	7	13	83		8,500,000
Italy	10	9	23	201	25,000	23,000,000
United States ...	16	23	29	53	20,000	64,000,000
Japan	8	10	22	93	24,000	29,000,000

1910

Country	Older Battleships	Dreadnoughts	Cruisers	Destroyers	Submarines	Personnel	Cost
Great Britain....	53	20	82	318	65	138,000	$165,000,000
France	16	2	43	305	81		65,000,000
Russia	14	4	14	204	35		50,000,000
Germany	20	14	41	164	12		110,000,000
Austria-Hungary .	9	3	9	61	12	13,000	12,500,000
Italy	18	4	22	104	12	32,500	34,000,000
United States	27	6	36	61	27	45,000	140,000,000
Japan	12	3	34	166	17		36,000,000

1914

Country	Older Battleships	Dreadnoughts	Cruisers	Destroyers	Submarines	Personnel	Cost
Great Britain	40	31	118	362	85	151,000	255,000,000
France	21	7	31	253	76		97,500,000
Russia	10	4	23	103	14	53,500	120,000,000
Germany	20	21	47	199	37	73,000	120,000,000
Austria-Hungary .	12	4	12	88	6	18,000	15,250,000
Italy	11	4	22	131	25	42,000	55,000,000
United States	24	12	26	69	34		143,500,000
Japan	16	4	33	86	13	47,500	47,500,000

BIBLIOGRAPHICAL NOTE

THE literature, in many languages, of pre-war diplomacy is enormous. In this notice attention will be called to some important books in English or available in English translations. For an extensive list of books in foreign languages as well as in English, *Foreign Affairs Bibliography, 1919-1932*, edited by William L. Langer and Hamilton Fish Armstrong (New York, 1933), may be profitably consulted. G. P. Gooch, *Recent Revelations of European Diplomacy* (3d edition, London and New York, 1930), offers an admirable summary of and commentary on the principal documentary collections, autobiographies and biographies published since the war. A briefer discussion will be found in S. B. Fay, *The Origins of the World War* (New York, 1928), vol. I, pp. 1-32.

STANDARD WORKS

Although written before most of the material now available was published, G. P. Gooch, *History of Modern Europe, 1878-1919* (London and New York, 1930), is still valuable. The most generally useful book is S. B. Fay, *The Origins of the World War* (2 vols., 2nd edition, New York, 1930), which, though sympathetic to the Central Powers, is written without passion or prejudice. H. E. Barnes, *The Genesis of the World War* (2nd edition, New York, 1927), offers an extreme statement of the case for the Central Powers. H. W. Wilson, *The War Guilt* (London, 1928) is strongly pro-*Entente*. R. J. Sontag, *European Diplomatic History, 1871-1932* (New York, 1933), may be recommended as a sound interpretation rather than as a narrative of events. J. S. Ewart, *The Roots and Causes of the Wars, 1914-1918*

(2 vols., New York, 1925), is a substantial work by a Canadian jurist.

For the period 1871-1890, W. L. Langer, *European Alliances and Alignments* (New York, 1931), vol. I, provides the best account, although J. V. Fuller, *Bismarck's Diplomacy at Its Zenith* (Cambridge, 1922) should not be neglected for the years 1885-1888. Langer's second volume will carry the story down to 1902. Until its publication, his earlier book *The Franco-Russian Alliance* (Cambridge, Mass., 1929) remains indispensable. G. Lowes Dickinson, *The International Anarchy, 1904-1914* (London and New York, 1926), has a mildly pacifist tinge, while R. B. Mowat, *The Concert of Europe* (London, 1930), is written from the point of view suggested by the title.

An orthodox presentation is found in Sir A. W. Ward and G. P. Gooch, *The Cambridge History of British Foreign Policy*, vol. III (Cambridge and New York, 1923), *1866-1919;* it may be compared with A. F. Pribram, *England and the International Policy of the European Great Powers, 1871-1914* (Oxford, 1931). The most objective books by Germans are Erich Brandenburg, *From Bismarck to the World War* (Oxford, 1927), and Otto Hammann, *The World Policy of Germany, 1890-1912* (New York, 1927). In default of an adequate study of French policy, E. M. Carroll, *French Public Opinion and Foreign Affairs, 1871-1914* (New York, 1931) may be consulted. G. H. Stuart, *French Foreign Policy from Fashoda to Serajevo, 1898-1914* (New York, 1921), is now somewhat out of date. A. F. Pribram, *The Secret Treaties of Austria-Hungary, 1879-1914* (2 vols., Cambridge, Mass., 1921, 1922) is indispensable, for it provides the texts of the treaties. The same author's *Austrian Foreign Policy, 1908-1918* (London, 1923) is inadequate, and so is Baron S. A. Korff, *Russia's Foreign Relations During the Last Half Century* (New York, 1922). There is no account available in English of Italian policy. M. Bogichevich, *Causes of the War* (Amsterdam, 1919), is highly critical of Serbian policy, although the author is himself a Serb.

E. N. Anderson, *The First Moroccan Crisis, 1904-1906* (Chicago, 1930), O. J. Hale, *Germany and the Diplomatic Revolution, 1904-1908* (Philadelphia, 1931), and O. H. Wedel, *Austro-German Diplomatic Relations, 1908-1914* (Stanford University, 1932), are excellent studies of their several subjects. E. M. Earle, *Turkey, the Great Powers and the Bagdad Railway* (New York, 1923) is still useful, although it was written before the most pertinent documents were published. Conflicting points of view are provided by M. E. Durham, *The Serajevo Crime* (London, 1925) and R. W. Seton-Watson, *Sarajevo* (1926); Bruno Brehm, *They Call It Patriotism* (Boston, 1932), though somewhat fictionalized, portrays the atmosphere of the crime in striking fashion.

For the crisis of July, 1914, the fullest account is B. E. Schmitt, *The Coming of the War 1914* (2 vols., New York, 1930); to which M. H. Cochran, *Germany Not Guilty in 1914* (Boston, 1931) is a reply. Sir Charles Oman, *The Outbreak of the War of 1914-1918* (London, 1919), is a semi-official British narrative. P. Renouvin, *The Immediate Origins of the War* (New Haven, 1928), is the classic French account. Much more critical is A. Fabre-Luce, *The Limitations of Victory* (New York, 1926). Count Max Montgelas, *The Case for the Central Powers* (London and New York, 1925) and A. von Wegerer, *A Refutation of the Versailles War Guilt Thesis* (New York, 1930), are the best presentations of the German point of view. K. Kautsky, *The Guilt of William Hohenzollern* (London, 1920) is highly critical of German policy. There are no accounts by Austrians, Russians or Serbs available in English. A. Salandra, *The Intervention of Italy* (London and New York, 1932) is an authoritative statement by the head of the government. Emil Ludwig, *July 1914* (New York, 1929) is not to be taken seriously, though the author undoubtedly meant to be serious. J. F. Scott, *Five Weeks*

(New York, 1927), provides a valuable survey of the newspaper press during the crisis.

Miscellaneous: C. J. H. Hayes, *Essays in Nationalism* (New York, 1926); *Historical Evolution of Modern Nationalism* (New York, 1931). P. T. Moon, *Imperialism and World Politics* (New York, 1927). H. Feis, *Europe the World's Banker, 1870-1914* (New Haven, 1931).

BIOGRAPHIES AND AUTOBIOGRAPHIES

Nearly all the statesmen, diplomatists, generals and admirals of the pre-war period have written their *apologiæ* or have been the subjects of biographies. The most important are, for Great Britain: Sir Sidney Lee, *Life of King Edward VII* (2 vols., London, 1925-1927); Lady G. Cecil, *Life of Robert Marquis of Salisbury* (4 vols., London, 1921-32); Lord Newton, *Lord Lansdowne: a Biography* (London, 1929); H. H. Asquith, *The Genesis of the War* (London, 1923); J. A. Spender and Cyril Asquith, *Life of Lord Oxford and Asquith* (2 vols., London, 1932); Viscount Grey of Fallodon, *Twenty-Five Years, 1892-1916* (2 vols., London, 1925), of which Hermann Lutz, *Lord Grey and the World War* (London, 1928), is a searching criticism; Lord Haldane, *Before the War* (London, 1920); Winston S. Churchill, *The World Crisis, 1911-1915* (London, 1923); David Lloyd George, *War Memoirs*, vol. I (London, 1933); Harold Nicolson, *Life of Lord Carnock* (London, 1930); H. Wickham Steed, *Through Thirty Years* (London, 1924); Sir George Buchanan, *My Mission to Russia* (2 vols., London, 1923).

For France: *The Memoirs of Raymond Poincaré* (4 vols., New York, 1926-28); M. Paléologue, *An Ambassador's Memoirs*, vol. I (New York, 1924); R. Viviani, *As We See It* (New York, 1923).

For Germany: William II, *My Memoirs* (New York, 1922); *Memoirs of Prince von Bülow* (4 vols., Boston, 1931-32), strongly colored and not always reliable, but none the less important; T. von Bethmann-Hollweg, *Reflections on the World War* (London, 1920); Admiral von Tirpitz, *My Memoirs* (2 vols., New York, 1919); Baron von Eckardstein, *Ten Years at the Court of St. James, 1895-1905* (New York, 1922); Prince Lichnowsky, *Heading for the Abyss* (New York, 1928); Baron von Schoen, *Memoirs of an Ambassador* (London, 1922); B. Huldermann, *Albert Ballin* (London, 1922).

For Austria-Hungary: Joseph Redlich, *The Emperor Francis Joseph* (New York, 1929); Albert Baron von Margutti, *The Emperor Francis Joseph and His Times* (London, 1921); J. M. Baernreither, *Fragments of a Political Diary* (New York, 1930), valuable for Austro-Serbian relations; Count Julius Andrássy, *Diplomacy and the War* (London, 1921).

For Russia: A. P. Izvolsky, *Recollections of a Foreign Minister* (Garden City, 1921), a fragment; F. Stieve, *Izvolsky and the World War* (New York, 1926), highly critical; S. D. Sazonov, *Fateful Years* (New York, 1928); Baron Rosen, *Forty Years of Diplomacy* (2 vols., New York, 1922); A. Nekludoff, *Diplomatic Reminiscences* (London, 1920); A. Savinsky, *Recollections of a Russian Diplomat* (London, 1927).

For Italy: G. Giolitti, *Memoirs of My Life* (London, 1923).

Miscellaneous: H. A. Gibbons, *Venizelos* (Boston, 1923); Djemal Pasha, *Memoirs of a Turkish Statesman, 1913-1919* (New York, 1922); I. E. Geshov, *The Balkan League* (London, 1915).

DOCUMENTS

The defeat of the Central Powers in the war caused the new governments in Germany and Austria to publish the diplomatic correspondence of the former régimes; in fact the Soviet government began to do this as early as 1917. Great Britain and France have been forced to follow the example thus set, and Italy and Yugoslavia (Serbia) have announced similar plans. Some documents have also been published privately. Close to 50,000 documents are now available to students of diplomatic history from 1871 to 1914, and the total may ultimately reach 100,000.

The more important collections are as follows:

Austria-Hungary: *Œsterreich-Ungarns Aussenpolitik von der Bosnischen Krise 1909 bis zum Kriegsausbruch 1914,* edited by L. Bittner, A. F. Pribram, etc. (8 vols., Vienna, 1930).

Diplomatische Aktenstücke zur Vorgeschichte des Krieges 1914 (3 vols., Vienna, 1919). English translation: *Official Files Relating to Pre-war History* (3 vols., London, 1920).

Belgium: *Amtliche Aktenstücke zur Geschichte der Europäischen Politik, 1885-1914,* edited by B. Schwertfeger (5 vols., Berlin, 1925). Belgian documents seized by the Germans during their occupation of Brussels.

France: *Documents diplomatiques français, 1871-1914,* edited by the Commission de Publication des Documents relatifs aux Origines de la Guerre de 1914 (Paris, 1929-   ), in three series, I, 1871-1900; II, 1901-1911; III, 1911-1914. Will probably comprise about 45 volumes.

Germany: *Die Grosse Politik der Europäischen Kabinette, 1871-1914,* edited by J. Lepsius, A. Mendelssohn Bartholdy, F. Thimme (40 vols., Berlin, 1922-27). Condensed English translation: *German Diplomatic Documents, 1871-1914,* edited by E. T. S. Dugdale (4 vols., New York, 1928-31).

Die deutschen Dokumente zum Kriegsausbruch, edited by M. Montgelas and W. Schücking (4 vols., Charlottenburg, 1919; 2nd edition, Berlin, 1927). English translation: *Outbreak of the World War: German documents collected by Karl Kautsky* (New York, 1924).

Great Britain: *British Documents on the Origins of the War, 1898-1914,* edited by G. P. Gooch and Harold

Temperley (London, 1926-   ), to be completed in 11 volumes.

Russia: *Materials for the Study of Franco-Russian Relations, 1910-1914,* in Russian (Moscow, 1922). French translation: *Un livre noir* (2 vols., Paris, 1922, 1923); German translation: *Der diplomatische Schriftwechsel Iswolskis,* edited by F. Stieve (4 vols., Berlin, 1924).

Entente Diplomacy and the World, edited by B. von Siebert and G. A. Schreiner (New York, 1922), unofficially published.

International Relations in the Epoch of Imperialism, in Russian, edited by M. N. Pokrovsky (Moscow, 1931-1934). German translation: *Die internationalen Beziehungen im Zeitalter des Imperialismus,* edited by Otto Hoetzsch (Berlin, 1931-34). Five volumes issued for the period from 14 January to 4 August, 1914; will cover the years 1878-1917.

How the War Began in 1914 (London, 1925). The diary of Baron Shilling, a high official of the Russian foreign office, for the crisis of 1914.

Serbia: *Die auswärtige Politik Serbiens, 1903-1914,* edited by M. Bogichevich (3 vols., Berlin, 1928-30), unofficially published.

Sarajevo: *Un drame historique: L'attentat de Sarajevo. Documents inédits et texte intégral des sténogrammes du procès,* edited by Albert Mousset (Paris, 1930). Minutes of the trial of the assassins of the Archduke Francis Ferdinand.

College students will find the following "source-books" convenient:

G. B. Manhart, *Alliance and Entente, 1871-1914* (New York, 1932).

W. H. Cooke and E. P. Stickney, *Readings in European International Relations since 1879* (New York, 1931).

Viscount Grey, *Speeches on Foreign Affairs, 1904-1914,* edited by P. Knaplund (Cambridge, Mass., 1932).

INDEX